GEMS OF WISDOM

GEMS OF WISDOM

from the
SEVENTH DALAI LAMA

Translation and commentary
by Glenn H. Mullin

Snow Lion
Boston & London

Snow Lion
An imprint of Shambhala Publications, Inc.
Horticultural Hall
300 Massachusetts Avenue
Boston, Massachusetts 02115
www.shambhala.com

Printed in the United States of America

⊗This edition is printed on acid-free paper that meets the
American National Standards Institute Z39.48 Standard.
♻Shambhala Publications makes every effort to print on recycled
paper. For more information please visit www.shambhala.com.
Distributed in the United States by Penguin Random House LLC
and in Canada by Random House of Canada Ltd

Library of Congress Cataloging-in-Publication Data
Bskal-bzaṅ-rgya-mtsho, Dalai Lama VII, 1708–1757.
[Dri len rin chen 'phreṅ ba. English]
Gems of wisdom from the Seventh Dalai Lama / translated and
with commentary by Glenn H. Mullin.
p. cm.
ISBN 978-1-55939-132-0 (alk. paper)
1. Spiritual life—Dge-lugs-pa (Sect). 2. Buddhist meditations.
I. Mullin, Glenn H. II. Title.
BQ7935.B75343 E5 1999
294.3'444—dc21
99-048048

Table of Contents

Introduction

The year was 1720. The Seventh Dalai Lama, whose ordination name was Gyalwa Kalzang Gyatso, was only twelve years old. He sat on the throne that had been prepared for him in the Jokhang, Tibet's oldest and most sacred temple, and waited for his first audience with the peoples of Central Tibet to begin. Although he had been recognized as the Sixth Dalai Lama's reincarnation more than a decade earlier, at the time Lhasa was under the occupation of hostile Mongol forces, and therefore his early education had begun in his homeland far to the east and away from the turmoil, first in Kham and then Amdo. The Mongol forces had recently been routed, and now he had been brought to Lhasa and enthroned in the Potala.

In Lhasa he had been placed in the traditional five-room apartment on the roof of the Potala that was reserved for the Dalai Lama incarnations. The building itself stood on Red Mountain, and towered over the city like a crown jewel. It was said to have almost a thousand rooms, although only the five on the roof were officially his. The floor below him housed Namgyal Dratsang, the monastery that had been established by his predecessor (four lifetimes earlier) the Third Dalai Lama, and had evolved to become the private monastery of future Dalai Lamas. Other rooms housed audience chambers, chapels, libraries and archives.

Like most buildings in Tibet, the Potala had a flat roof. His apartment opened onto a section of this that served as a large patio, and from here he could look out over the entire city. (This is the same rooftop courtyard depicted in the film *Kundun*, with His Holiness the present Dalai Lama as a youth looking out through a telescope.) His view took in a dozen of Lhasa's temples and monasteries, and also the mighty Kyichu River that flowed into the valley from the west and exited eastward. The Lhasa Valley was rimmed in on the north and south by mountains, and those on the north were dotted with monasteries, nunneries, temples and retreat hermitages, their faces turned to the warm southern sun. He had marveled at the spectacle that morning, before leaving for the Jokhang.

The city itself was in a mood of celebration. The Mongol forces that had held Lhasa for almost fifteen years had now been pushed out. Tibet was once more an independent nation, and their treasured Dalai Lama had been brought home. He was to give a public blessing for the first time that day, and thousands of people had lined up long before the sun had even risen. He leaned ahead on the throne that had been erected in the large courtyard in front of the main chapel of the Jokhang, and the long line began to make its way to where he sat. First came all the high lamas, then the kings, chieftains and their families, then the monks and nuns, and finally all and sundry. In his hand he held a small blessing wand, and he touched the head of each pilgrim with it as they filed past him. For a twelve-year-old boy born of humble stock in a rural area of eastern Tibet, it was quite a day.

Soon, however, this celebratory phase of his life was over, and was replaced by the strict regime of his spiritual education. He was to excel in this and go on to become one of the greatest Dalai Lamas in the history of the lineage.

As an adult, the Seventh Dalai Lama became a prolific writer. An enthusiast of Tantric Buddhism, many of his literary endeavors are dedicated to his favorite tantric practices. These generally are highly technical in style, and are intended for initiates only. Indeed, their language is steeped in tantric symbolism to the degree that few non-initiates would be able to access their meaning. Tibetans call this type of literature "self-secret." Many of the tantric works of the Seventh are hundreds of pages in length, and reveal the tremendous depth of his spiritual learning and accomplishment. They also, of course, point to lineages of tantric transmission that he himself held. Texts in this genre are usually written at the request of a particular disciple or patron, and provide guidelines in specific tantric practices.

The work that serves as the focus of this volume, however, was created for an entirely different audience. Here the Seventh addresses the key elements of spiritual life from a universal perspective. His medium naturally is the Buddhist linguistic environment, for he himself had been a Buddhist monk from the years of his early childhood. In other words, he speaks as a Buddhist monk on what he sees as being the most fundamental spiritual issues that confront us as human beings.

He writes in verse, and the style is one of question and answer. Each verse is four lines in length, with the question posed in the first two lines and the answer provided in the last two. In total the text is 108 verses in length, an auspicious number in Tibetan Buddhism. He complements these with two introductory and two concluding verses.

He often brings humor into his writing, for Tibetans love to laugh. It could almost be called their national pastime. One verse, for example, asks the question, "What is like a smelly fart, that, although invisible, is obvious?" His reply: "One's own faults, that are precisely as obvious as the effort made to hide them." And in another verse he asks, "What is the body odor easy to acquire but hard to lose?" He replies by saying, "Habits picked up from people whose lives are far from truth."

In a concluding verse to the text he states,

> I wrote this song
> Of useful hints from the tongues of sages
> Arranged as a precious string of jewels....

In other words, he is not claiming to be the inventor of the spiritual teachings embodied in his text. Rather, what he has done is draw from the teachings of the great Buddhist masters of the past, including the Buddha himself; the early Indian Buddhist masters such as Nagarjuna, Aryadeva, Asanga, Vasubandhu, Shantideva and Atisha; and also the great Tibetan lamas such as Milarepa, Sakya Pandita, Lama Tsongkhapa, and the early Dalai Lama and Panchen Lama incarnations. Thus in this quintessential text he assembles the collective wisdom of more than 2,000 years of Buddhist history.

The work is a wonderful and practical little guide to the spiritual values cherished by Buddhists everywhere. The Seventh Dalai Lama's words are a source of spiritual inspiration for anyone who reads them with an open mind. Many of these are common to people of all spiritual traditions, and many Christian readers will find that the spirituality hinted at by the Seventh Dalai Lama holds many values that are recommended by Jesus and his followers. Similarly, Muslims, Hindus, Taoists and Confucians, to name but a few, will recognize that many of the truths deemed spiritually relevant by the Seventh Dalai Lama are also echoed in various forms within their own spiritual traditions.

The collection to which the Seventh's text is attached is entitled *A Well-Arranged Collection of Songs and Verses of Spiritual Advice Connected with the Lojong Tradition*. This compilation contains thirty-eight verse works on spiritual experience and the path to enlightenment written by the Seventh at different periods of his life, but only brought together and published after his death.

A note in the collection states that the text is one of five included in the anthology that were "not written at the request of a disciple," but rather "are spontaneous creations of Gyalwa Kalzang Gyatso's pen." The same note goes on to say that these five have no dates nor place names associated with their writing, but that each of them was "composed in a single session, and not one word of them thereafter changed from the way it originally appeared." The note concludes by stating, "Small in size but profound in meaning, they are extremely useful for anyone interested in spiritual development." That note, of course, was written by the lama who compiled the collection many years subsequent to their composition, i.e., after the Seventh's passing in 1757. In all probability this was Changkya Rolpai Dorje, a monk from Amdo, northeastern Tibet, who was the Seventh's main spiritual heir and also, incidentally, a tutor to the family of the Manchu Emperor.

The Tibetan term *Lojong* in the above title means "spiritual transformation," or alternatively "training the mind." The nature of texts classified as Lojong is that they should contribute directly and immediately to spiritual transformation. The term has its origins in the lineages of Indonesian Buddhism brought to Tibet in 1042 by the Indian master Atisha Dipamkara Shrijnana. Atisha had studied Buddhism in many of the great monasteries of India, but became disillusioned by its emphasis on academic fluff. Rumors reached him telling of the more vibrant forms that Buddhism had taken in Indonesia. Consequently he made the long and perilous sea journey to that land, where he remained for twelve years under the spiritual tutorage of an Indonesian sage known to Tibetans as Serlingpa Chokyi Drakpa, or (in Sanskrit) Suvarnadvipi Dharmakirti, "He Famed for Truth (from the) Golden Islands."

The differences in the approaches to Buddhism that he encountered in India and Indonesia profoundly impressed him, and he became an advocate of the latter. Most of his lineages from Indonesia became known as Lojong, or "Mind-Transforming." The implication, of course, was that the more academic Buddhism of India was not as directly transformative for an individual practitioner as were the Indonesian lineages.

Atisha's Lojong lineages from Indonesia were gradually absorbed by all schools of Tibetan Buddhism. The character of this tradition was that it stripped away all the academic obsessions that surrounded the Buddhism of eleventh-century India and reduced Dharma to quintessential contemplative practice based on oral transmission. The Kadampa school that descended from Atisha and his chief disciple Lama Drom Tonpa (a predecessor of the Dalai Lamas) became famed in Tibet for the manner in which it used contemplative practice and simple living as defined by the Indonesian Buddhists (as transmitted to Atisha by Serlingpa) as the basis of training, and used the academic traditions of India as complementary studies while pursuing the contemplative life. Therefore Lama Dronpa said, "Whenever I study I also contemplate and meditate. Whenever I contemplate

I also study and meditate. And when I meditate I also study and contemplate. This is the Kadampa way."

The emphasis on oral tradition over academic study was recommended by Atisha himself when he was once asked, "What is the best approach to the Dharma: the study of a vast field of scriptures, or application to a quintessential oral transmission lineage?" He endorsed the latter, and thus revealed his reverence for essential practice. He held the practice-oriented lineages received from his Indonesian master Serlingpa Dharmakirti in far greater esteem than the more academically oriented Indian lineages received earlier in his life. Tears are said to have come to his eyes whenever he mentioned the name of this great guru.

The present work by the Seventh Dalai Lama embodies the key themes of this practice tradition, with all teachings of the Buddha brought into the context of their implications for individual transformation, or "the training of the mind," as the Lojong tradition puts it.

The Sixth Dalai Lama had passed away in 1706. In accordance with tradition, a committee was formed shortly thereafter, empowered with the task of overseeing the search for his reincarnation. The focus of the search turned to the regions of Eastern Tibet near the border with China, for all prophecies of the State Oracle of Nechung Monastery, and the visions seen in the Oracle Lake at Lhamo Latso, pointed in this direction.

In 1709 a young boy exhibiting all the signs of being the true reincarnation was found in Litang, Kham. The child had been born in 1708 near a monastery constructed by the Third Dalai Lama a century and a half earlier. He was tested and then formally recognized as the Seventh incarnation. Soon thereafter a team of high lamas was sent from Lhasa to initiate and oversee his spiritual education and training.

The Seventh spent his early life in the monasteries of Eastern Tibet, first at Litang Monastery and then later at Kumbum in Amdo. Both of these monasteries had been built by the Third Dalai Lama in the late 1400s, and thus were closely linked to the

Dalai Lama incarnations. His spiritual tutors from Lhasa moni-
tored his growth and training closely, and he received a steady
stream of spiritual teachings and initiations.

This continued until he was twelve years old, when in 1720
he was taken to Lhasa and enthroned in the Potala. There he
continued with his rigorous training, guided by some of the
most famous lamas in the country. During this period he received an almost endless stream of lineage transmissions. As
his Tibetan biography by Changkya Rolpai Dorje puts it, "There
was not a single teaching coming from the Buddha, neither in
the sutra nor tantra fields, that he did not receive and master."
His day began with long hours of meditation, followed by many
classes of instruction and debate. This was coupled with peri-
odic retreats.

By the time he reached his late twenties the Seventh Dalai
Lama had completed his training and achieved spiritual realization, becoming a spiritual master equal to any of the Dalai Lama
incarnations before him. He dedicated the remainder of his life
to teaching, writing and the practice of meditation.

His writings stand as some of the most profoundly spiritual
literature to emerge from the Land of Snows, achieving an ease
of style and clarity of delivery that won them an instant audience throughout Central Asia. Their popularity remains as
strong today, two and a half centuries later. He is remembered
in history as one of the most profoundly spiritual lamas of his
era.

What perhaps is most surprising about his life, though, is
that he turned out as he did; for he lived in tumultuous times. It
is a credit to his tutors that they were able to keep him out of
the political chaos of the day and instead focussed on the spiritual life.

The early Dalai Lamas had, of course, set the stage for the
shape the Seventh's life was to take; for he was recognized as
being their reincarnation, and thus from childhood was trained
to assume the mantle of their works.

The First Dalai Lama had been born in 1391, became a monk at the age of seven, and achieved spiritual realization by his mid-twenties, becoming the guru of many of the most important personalities of his day. In particular he spent much of his adult life travelling and teaching throughout Southwestern Tibet, and the monastery he built near Shigatse, Tashi Lhunpo by name, quickly became one of the most important spiritual institutions in the country.

His reincarnation, born in late 1475, continued the work of the First, but travelled and taught most extensively in Central and Southern Tibet, establishing monasteries and meditation retreat facilities throughout these regions. As his biography states, "By the time he had become an old man there was hardly a person in the entire region between China and Kashmir who had not become his disciple." Chokhor Gyal, the monastery he established at Metoktang below the Oracle Lake, was to become an important link with subsequent Dalai Lama incarnations, for visions in it would always be a criterion in the search for all of his future reincarnations. He passed away in 1542 amid many miraculous signs and omens.

The Third continued the work of the Second, and during his life travelled and taught extensively, especially in the Mongol regions to the north and also in the east along Tibet's border with China. As we saw earlier, the Seventh Dalai Lama was later to spend several of his childhood years in two of the monasteries built by the Third, firstly in the southeast at Litang, and then in the northeast at Kumbum. No doubt this connection, coming so early in his life, instilled within him a strong sense of respect for the exalted history associated with the Dalai Lama office, and also an awe for the destiny that lay before him.

The Fourth was the only Dalai Lama not to be born in Tibet. He had taken birth in a Mongol aristocratic family descended directly from Genghis Khan. According to his biography, his blood link was nineteen generations removed in decent from the Great Genghis. For the Tibetans this was a symbol of the role of the Dalai Lamas. The Third had visited and taught extensively in Mongolia, introducing the basic foundations of the gentle Buddhist message. Now his reincarnation the Fourth would take this seed to fulfillment. Genghis had brought the

Mongols war and tyranny, but the Fourth Dalai Lama would bring them to the path of peace and enlightenment. Indeed, Mongolia has on the whole remained committed to the pursuit of Tibetan Buddhist ideals from then until the present day.

Each of the four early Dalai Lamas had belonged to the Gelukpa, or Yellow Hat, school of Tibetan Buddhism. The Fifth Dalai Lama took birth in an important family belonging to the Nyingma, or Old School. The events of his day would make this choice of parenthood significant. During his lifetime Tibet broke out in civil war, with Mongol factions coming in on both sides. At the conclusion of the turmoil the powerbrokers of Central Asia felt that aristocratic rule was no longer effective in Tibet, with its complex structure of tribes and clans. They looked back in history to when, four hundred years earlier, the Mongol king Kublai Khan had subjugated both Tibet and China, and then given Tibet its independence under the rule of the head lamas of the Sakya school. The Tibetans remembered this era as one of peace and prosperity, and felt that such a structure could once again be put in place. A high lama would have connections to all tribes and clans due to Tibet's complex structure of monastic education. The Fifth Dalai Lama was a natural choice for the position; his predecessors had travelled and taught extensively throughout almost all regions of Central Asia, not only in Tibet but also in Mongolia and Western China. Because of this the Dalai Lama office had established spiritual connections throughout the land and commanded tremendous respect among the general population of Tibetans. Moreover, most of Tibet's aristocratic families belonged to the Nyingma school, and the Fifth Dalai Lama had been born into a powerful Nyingmapa family. This gave him the confidence of the Nyingmapa aristocrats, without which no Tibetan leader could succeed. The outcome was that in 1642 the Fifth Dalai Lama was enthroned as the spiritual and temporal head of Tibet, a position into which all subsequent reincarnations were born.

It should be understood, however, that although all Dalai Lamas were expected to play an important spiritual role, the position of secular leadership was largely symbolic. All the Fifth Dalai Lama did in the secular sphere was participate in the creation of the structure by which Tibet was to operate, and thereafter retired to a spiritual life for the remainder of his life, which in his case took the form of amazingly voluminous writing. The Seventh and Eighth were directly involved in secular government for only brief periods of their lives. Not until the Thirteenth Dalai Lama did a Dalai Lama take up the mantle of secular governance, and he only did so when forced by the circumstances of firstly the 1904 invasion of Tibet by Great Britain and then the 1909 invasion by Chinese forces. From the time Tibet regained her independence in 1913 until his death in 1933 he personally directed many of the affairs of state.

To give a better sense of this aspect of a Dalai Lama's life it is useful to understand that the Lhasa government, established during the life of the Fifth Dalai Lama and continued over the centuries to follow, was not a hands-on undertaking. Tibet under the Dalai Lamas was a federation of several hundred kingdoms and tribes, each with its own king or chieftain, as well as local head lama, who usually was the reincarnation of some ancient sage associated with generations gone by. The principal role of the Dalai Lama was that of peacemaker, and the role of the Lhasa government one of facilitator. There are a few brief periods in Tibetan history when this was not the case, but it generally held true. The occasions in which the Lhasa government played a bigger role were generally inspired by external conditions, such as invasion by hostile forces.

During the lifetime of the Sixth Dalai Lama, however, things almost fell apart. He himself was much of a bystander to the events that occurred, for he was too young to partake in them. The administration of Tibet was being conducted by the very able prime minister installed during the Fifth Dalai Lama's elder years, Desi Sangye Gyatso by name. This extraordinary man had facilitated and overseen the emergence of the New Tibet. Unfortunately for him, when the Sixth was still a youth, civil war broke out in Mongolia and spilled over into the Land of Snows. In 1703 Lhazang Khan of the Qoshot Mongols invaded Lhasa, put Desi Sangye Gyatso to death, captured the young Sixth Dalai Lama and in 1706 placed a puppet on the Dalai Lama throne. The Sixth died the following year under mysterious circumstances.

Thus when the Seventh Dalai Lama was born in Litang in 1708 it was into a Tibet under foreign occupation, and with a puppet Dalai Lama on the throne. When the child from Litang was recognized in 1709 as the Sixth's reincarnation, there was considerable concern for his immediate safety. Lhazang Khan naturally viewed the recognition of the boy as a rejection of the lama he had enthroned in Lhasa and as the potential focus of a resistance movement to his rule. However, other events in Central Asia contrived against the Mongol warlord's tenure. A Tibetan resistance movement had allied itself with the Dzungar Mongols and begun to attack the Qoshot forces with success. In 1717 Lhazang Khan's army was routed and expelled.

The Dzungar soldiers proved to be as much of a curse as a blessing, and after the Qoshots were eliminated they engaged in a free-for-all campaign of pillaging and looting. In particular they chose monasteries of the Nyingma school as the object of their greed, for these, having received the patronage of the Nyingma aristocracy for centuries, were rich in statues and religious objects made of gold and other precious substances.

Meanwhile far to the east the young Seventh Dalai Lama lived a quiet monastic life, with the emphasis being strongly placed on his spiritual education. He was being carefully kept out of the many intrigues that were underfoot, and was being prepared for the day when he could be brought forth and held up as the symbol of a unified and independent Tibet.

For the five hundred years prior to the birth of the Seventh Dalai Lama, Mongolia had stood strong as the sole superpower of Central Asia, and its empire surpassed in size even that of the ancient Romans. At one point in its history Mongolia ruled everything from Constantinople to Korea, and its armies wandered wherever they so willed almost without resistance. However, as all empires must, theirs was coming to an end. Times were changing, and a new star was rising in the east. The Manchus had invaded and captured China, and established their capital in Beijing. The Manchu emperor took a strong interest in the Mongol wars, for their outcome would strongly affect the stability of his own western border regions.

Moreover, he held a double interest in Tibet. The first of these was born from the fact that Tibetan Buddhism was now a major force throughout Central Asia, not only in Tibet and Mongolia, but also in Northern India, Manchuria and many regions of China. Whoever held the seat of the Dalai Lama would hold a strong sway over the hearts of the millions of peoples populating these areas; anyone befriending the Dalai Lama would win the favor and trust of those millions. The Emperor could only benefit from close ties with the Dalai Lama.

But there was also a directly spiritual side to the Emperor's intent. He himself had been born into a family that practiced the Dalai Lama's school of Tibetan Buddhism, and he held a strong concern for the outcome of events for purely spiritual reasons. And now the child recognized by the high Tibetan lamas as being the reincarnation of the Sixth Dalai Lama had taken birth just a few miles from his own borders! He immediately sent a delegation to Litang with gifts and congratulations, and also with the pledge of an annual stipend to carry the boy through the period of difficulty, i.e., the disruption of his life caused by the Mongol wars.

This seemingly small event led to a growing friendship between the Seventh Dalai Lama and the Manchu emperor. This further blossomed in 1716, when the child was eight years old. The Manchu ruler requested the guardians of the young incarnation to take their ward from Litang to Kumbum Monastery, and offered to foot the bill. Events in Central Tibet had recently taken a turn for the worse, with the Qoshot and Dzungars going at one another in full force; the Emperor felt that Kumbum would be a much safer residence for the boy, for its location was such that he could personally provide Manchu forces for protection should the Mongol wars spread eastward. The Tibetans accepted, and Kumbum became the new residence of the young Dalai Lama.

Life here was more dramatic for the young lama, for Kumbum was accessible to hundreds of peoples of the northeast. His studies were regularly interspersed with visits from high lamas of the outlying regions, as well as entire tribes and clans in search of his blessings. To the Tibetans, even though he was not yet a teenager, he nonetheless carried in his presence the full blessing power of the entire line of Dalai Lama incarnations. The turmoil that at the time filled the valleys of Central Tibet must have seemed to him a long way away.

From this time onward Tibetan history took a deciding turn. Tibet's centuries-old pact with Mongolia, established in the times of Genghis and Godan Khan, had been shattered by the recent Mongol wars. By 1720 these had subsided and Tibet had regained its independence. It was time to bring the young Seventh Dalai Lama to Lhasa and enthrone him in the Potala.

Getting the child safely to Central Tibet, however, was no easy task, for it was a journey requiring many months of travel over roads where disorientated fragments of the Mongol armies could be encountered at any turn. The Manchu ruler requested the Tibetans to allow him to send a protective force with the young lama's entourage to ensure their safe arrival, and also to send a delegation to make offerings at the enthronement ceremony. The Tibetans accepted.

For better or worse, this simple gesture was a major stone in the edifice eventually leading to Tibet becoming a protectorate of the Manchu dynasty. The relationship of *Cho Yon*, or "Patron/Priest," that Tibet had enjoyed with Mongolia for almost five centuries, was now transferred to Manchu China.

As said earlier, the Manchu ruler himself had both a political and a spiritual interest in Tibet. Politically he wanted the stability that a close relationship with the Dalai Lamas would bring, and spiritually he was a Tibetan Buddhist in the same school as the Dalai Lamas. Many Tibetan writers today suspect that he may have placed greater emphasis on the first of the above two concerns, but this is not borne out by the evidence. At least one of his sons became a Tibetan Buddhist monk under the Dalai Lama's tutorage, a gesture that the emperor would not have made lightly nor solely for political reasons. Moreover, he and his successor sponsored the translation and publication of thousands of texts from Tibetan into Manchu, Chinese and Mongolian, and sponsored the construction of hundreds of

Tibetan Buddhist monasteries and temples within the Chinese mainland. It is hard to imagine that all this was done simply as a disinterested token of good will.

The fact of the matter is that the friendship between Tibet and Manchu China that emerged during this period served both sides equally well, and there is little reason to suspect it of being a mere union of expedience. It survived from 1720 until 1911, when the Manchu Dynasty fell in China. The Manchus had been Tibetan Buddhists and thus the Tibetans trusted them in the Patron/Priest relationship. The revolution in China that saw the end of the Manchu Dynasty also saw the end of everything that the Tibetans held dear about their large neighbor to the east. In 1911 the Thirteenth Dalai Lama intensely down-scaled relations with China, and in 1913 cut off formal diplomatic ties completely and expelled all Chinese officials from within Tibet's borders. The era that had emerged during the life of the Seventh Dalai Lama and survived for almost two centuries was officially at an end.

Although the Seventh Dalai Lama was surrounded by such happenings during his early life, it seems that they did not distort his upbringing in any significant way, other than perhaps to make him somewhat cynical of worldly affairs. The turmoil of his times was kept at a safe distance and he was immersed in the spiritual training expected of a Dalai Lama, with the emphasis placed upon his religious life. His early years passed in study and meditation, while the spheres of secular concern were handled by the elders of Lhasa. By his late twenties he had achieved spiritual realization, and he went on to dedicate the remainder of his life to teaching, writing and in general uplifting the spiritual life of Central Asia. When he passed away in 1757, Tibet mourned the death of the monk who had perhaps been the greatest of all the Dalai Lama incarnations.

The present work by the Seventh Dalai Lama is a wonderful example of his spiritual message, and also of his understated humor. It uses worldly metaphors to illustrate key points in the enlightenment tradition, with subtle laughter lying in the juxtapositioning of the individual worldly images used and the meanings given to them. This is a gentle humor, of course, not designed to bring wild guffaws of laughter within readers, but rather is a warm wave flowing as an undercurrent through the text. No doubt part of it lies in the mere fact of a Dalai Lama saying the words. All of the vast and profound teachings of the Buddha, as well as of all earlier Buddhist masters of India and Tibet, are elucidated through similes and metaphors that employ such earthy images as smelly farts, body odor, wild horses, slimy monsters, mindless lunatics and so forth.

The work is essentially spiritual in nature. His usage of similes and metaphors, two literary devices given great attention in Tibetan poetry, also demonstrates the depth of his training in the Indian Buddhist classics.

He writes in verse, and any educated Tibetan would be able to access the full gist of his meaning. However, Tibetan literature is rich in the uniqueness of the Buddhist linguistic environment. Consequently the average Western reader could miss out on much of what is being said. I have taken the liberty of adding a few paragraphs of commentary at the bottom of each verse, in the hope that by doing so the richness of the Seventh Dalai Lama's work will become more accessible. Hopefully this will facilitate the reading for non-specialists.

Every verse in the Seventh Dalai Lama's text is intended as a small contemplation. A Tibetan would read a passage, and then sit quietly with it for a few moments in order to drink in its implications for his or her own spiritual life.

For this reason I have set each verse on its own page. The full range of Tibetan Buddhism is presented in a few carefully chosen words, and with a sentiment that is at once accessible and universal.

As the Seventh himself puts it in a closing verse,

> What is delusional and what is not?
> To show their difference I wrote this song....

The delusional states to which he is referring are obvious in his text. All ordinary beings have both wisdom and delusion within themselves; and all also have the potential to transcend the delusions and stabilize wisdom. The degree to which we engage in this process determines the level of inner peace and joy that we will achieve with our life, and the degree of benefit and happiness that we will bring to self and others.

Buddhism emphasizes the doctrine of non-duality. Ultimately there is no delusion and no wisdom, for these are merely relative phenomena established solely by mental imputation, and having only a conventional existence based on the laws of interdependent origination. All objects of knowledge exist only in relation to other things, and thus have no inherent or separate existence. Delusion is only a relatively appearing phenomenon, as is wisdom. Nonetheless happiness and suffering, the respective products of wisdom and delusion, seem very real and substantial to the experiencer, and so do their underlying causes, the forces of light and darkness that we bring into play in our lives.

The Seventh Dalai Lama's little text focusses upon the meeting place of these two levels of reality—conventional and ultimate—and upon how the flows that manifest on the conventional level of reality can be directed so as to create outer and inner environments within which the ultimate level of reality is easily perceived.

Gems of Wisdom:
Translation and Commentary

Prologue

With single-pointed devotion I bow down to
Guru Manjushri, the Ever-Youthful One, the
supreme deity, the spiritual doctor who
serves as an elixir to all beings, bringing
them happiness and goodness; himself being
a moon full with the all-knowing wisdom,
having forever abandoned the faults of every
samsaric imperfection.

All Tibetan texts begin with a passage of homage. This tradition was established by the early Tibetan translators in the seventh and eighth centuries, and has remained in vogue ever since.
The subject to which the homage is made indicates the type of
text that is to follow.

Here the homage is made to Manjushri, the Bodhisattva of
Wisdom. He is depicted holding a sword in his right hand that
represents the insight into the great void nature of things, a realization that cuts out the very root of ignorance concerning the
nature of the self. In his left hand he holds a book, representing
knowledge of the methods for arousing this profound experience.

He is called the "Ever-Youthful One," for through this wisdom one achieves the perennial knowledge by which eternal happiness is attained. This empowers the recipient with the joyful
enthusiasm and vitality of a sixteen-year-old, and hence is called
"ever-youthful." He is also called "the supreme deity," for this
wisdom brings supreme liberation.

He is a "spiritual doctor who serves as an elixir to all beings," for this wisdom cures the anguish of the spirit and heals
the misery of conditioned existence. It is "an elixir," for its cure
extends to all spheres of one's life; the beyond-self wisdom benefits one in all matters mundane and spiritual.

Thus by dedicating his text to Manjushri, the Seventh
Dalai Lama indicates that his focus will be the wisdom of
enlightenment.

A magician manifests a double;
one becomes two;
a questioner and an answerer appear
and string this rosary of precious gems.

Every Tibetan text follows the opening homage with a passage known as "the promise of composition." In other words, the author declares what he intends to write about. Again, this is a tradition established by the early Buddhist masters and honored by all who followed in their wake.

Here the Seventh Dalai Lama declares that he will split himself into two, with one part serving as questioner and the other as responder. Together they will "string a rosary of precious jewels," meaning that the two will discuss the enlightenment path. This is a "string of precious gems," for spiritual knowledge is the most precious of all possessions acquirable by human beings.

By using the expression "a rosary of precious jewels," the Seventh reveals one of his primary sources of inspiration, the second-century Indian master Nagarjuna, whose text *The Ratnavali*, or *Rosary of Precious Gems*, has remained a great classic with Tibetans over the centuries. His Holiness the present Dalai Lama has publicly taught this scripture by Nagarjuna on numerous occasions.

1

What is the great ocean
most difficult to leave forever?
The three realms of cyclic existence,
which toss in waves of pain.

The "three realms of cyclic existence" refers to the three dimensions of unenlightened life, known as the realm of the senses
(or realm of desire), the realm of form and the realm of form-
lessness. These realms are only unenlightened, of course, when
experienced by an unenlightened being. They are often referred
to collectively as "the wheel of life," for living beings circle
through them from rebirth to rebirth until they eventually learn
the lessons of life and achieve enlightenment.

The first of the three is comprised of the six realms of ordinary rebirth: the hells, ghost realms, animal world (including
insects, fish, etc.), human world, world of the titans, and realm
of the sense gods. Each of these is associated with one of the
six root delusions or afflicted emotions. Respectively these are
anger, attachment, instinctual behavior, arrogance, jealousy, and
complacence.

Above these six realms are the seventeen god realms of form,
likened to seventeen stages of meditative absorption; and, above
these, the four realms of the formless gods, likened to formless
stages of meditative absorption. High meditators who have not
penetrated to the essence of wisdom are reborn into them.

Metaphorically the six realms of the sensory world represent cyclic processes resulting from the six distorted mind-states;
the form level gods represent mental activity that, although
profound, mistakes the nature of self; and the formless realms
represent exalted spiritual mind-states in which the fruits of

highest wisdom have not yet been achieved. In other words, the various realms are not only a map to the dimensions of rebirth, but also to everyday human experience.

2

What is the powerful glue that binds us
to the unpleasant environs of worldliness?
Sensory fixations, which cling with attachment
to the enticing things of the world.

This and the four verses that follow introduce the five root *klesha*, or "crazy darknesses" of the mind, the emotional and cognitive distortions that are the root of cyclic behavior and the sources of all unhappiness and suffering. The first of these listed by the Seventh Dalai Lama is attachment.

The Tibetan word for this klesha is *du chak. Du* means a sense of longing or wanting, and implies a *du-yon*, or object of the senses. *Chak* carries a suggestion of stickiness. In other words, it is a mind state that views an object of the five senses with a sticky obsession. We often see this translated as "desire," an English word that has a strong sexual implication and thus is really not very accurate.

Buddha spoke of sensory fixations as being the most pervasive cause of suffering. Because of them a person enters into states of mind in which happiness is dependent upon the objects or situations of the obsession. That person then experiences stress and anxiety in relation to the object. A general sense of discontent sets in, and he or she proceeds to adopt courses of action designed to satisfy this perceived indispensable need, harming those who seem to threaten it and manipulating those who seem to reinforce it.

Buddha spoke of sensory fixations as being like a drop of oil placed at the center of a sheet of paper. The oil slowly spreads over the paper, until it has pervaded the entire sheet. In the same way, unless we check our sensory addictions, they soon come to dominate our concerns, and our priorities take a self-destructive shift in focus.

In another of his poems the Seventh Dalai Lama speaks of the satisfaction experienced from feeding a sensory fixation as being "a huge loss for a small gain."

3

W̶hat is the great fire that rages
when we approach too closely to others?
Terrible anger that cannot bear
even the smallest challenge.

The second of the root klesha is anger. Sensory fixation may be the most pervasive destroyer of human happiness, but anger is the most immediate. One cannot experience anger and happiness in the same moment of time. When the heat of anger rises, the waters of happiness instantly evaporate. Anger by itself is a kind of spiritual pain.

As a result of anger the world engages in endless streams of harmful activity. When anger controls the mind, common sense and wisdom no longer operate. The person does foolish things, striking out violently at whatever is close, and thus destroying the happiness of self and others.

The great Indian master Shantideva wrote, "There is no negativity as strong as anger, and no spiritual practice as important as the discipline of restraint from it." And also, "The person who understands that anger is the real enemy and works with persistence to overcome it, and who does not identify enemies as external, finds happiness in this life and in whatever follows thereafter."

In Tantric Buddhism, anger is said to be connected with chemical activity in the crown chakra, i.e., the brain. Every time we allow anger to arise we send poisonous chemicals from the brain into the bloodstream and thereby into the entire body. Soon the release of these chemicals becomes a habit. Not only is one's state of consciousness profoundly impaired by them, in addition they give rise to a host of physical diseases. In other words, as well as harming the soul, anger harms our health.

4

What is the thick darkness obscuring
the truth before our very eyes?
Ignorance, that has existed
since time without beginning.

Here the Seventh Dalai Lama uses the word *ma rigpa*, or "ignorance." This refers specifically to misapprehension of the nature of the self. All other problems arise from not understanding the nature of the self.

"Self" in this sense has two applications: the deepest nature
of one's own continuum of being; and the deepest nature of all
other phenomena. To transcend emotional and cognitive distortions, together with the suffering that results from them, one
must arouse the profound wisdom that understands the final
nature of self and phenomena.

The Buddha used the term *anatma*, or "non-self," to refer to
these ultimate natures. He also used the term *shunyata*, which
means emptiness or voidness. We must arouse the wisdom that
appreciates the emptiness, or void-nature, of both the person
and phenomena.

The third-century Indian master Chandrakirti likened the
wisdom of emptiness to the eyes that guide us to enlightenment; all other spiritual practices he likened to the legs. With
strong legs and clear eyes we can travel to enlightenment quickly
and safely. We will see the Seventh's reference to this famous
metaphor later, in verse one hundred and seven.

Describing the object that is the focus of wisdom the Second
Dalai Lama wrote, "As for the object of the view (i.e., emptiness),
it is not made artificial by conditions, in essence is unchanging,

by nature is pristine, is beyond concepts of good and evil, is all-pervading, is the ultimate nature of all things and is the quintessence of the essence. Understanding it, one passes beyond the confines of confusion."

5

What is the wild horse that throws one
from the mountain one is ascending?
Pride which thinks oneself superior
and dwells on one's own good qualities.

The fourth of the five root klesha is pride. The Seventh Dalai
Lama likens it to "a wild horse that throws one from the mountain one is ascending," for it undermines one by transforming
one's blessings into weaknesses. One ascends the mountains of
life by means of one's strengths and talents, but pride causes
these very qualities to become negative. Of all forms of pride,
that arising from spiritual accomplishments is the worst.

The first three of the five root klesha are known as "the
three psychic poisons," for they poison one's life in a very direct
and immediate way. Pride is slightly more subtle. It is a negative
quality arising from positive ones. For example, one may be intelligent, but if one takes pride in this fact one's intelligence
becomes vain. One may be physically strong, but pride in one's
strength will only arouse ridicule. And one may be proud of
one's spiritual learning and endeavors, but pride causes the benefits to go to the wrong place. It strips the good quality of its
full force and distorts the manner in which that quality ripens.

Lama Tsongkhapa, the guru of the First Dalai Lama, likened good qualities to stilts that lift one up above ordinariness.
Pride makes one's movements on the stilts wobbly and dangerous to self and others.

6

Who is the mischievous slanderer
causing one to part from close friends?
Painful jealousy, that is unable to bear
the joy or success of others.

The fifth of the five root klesha is jealousy. Again, like pride, it arises from positive qualities. However, whereas pride arises from over-reacting to one's own strengths or endowments, jealousy arises from misinterpreting those of others.

The Seventh Dalai Lama calls it a "malicious slanderer," for just as slander creates distance, enmity and mistrust between living beings, jealousy causes distance, enmity and mistrust between oneself and those beings who have qualities that one admires. It causes one to "part from close friends," for one sees good qualities more easily in friends, but when jealousy arises as a result, the overall effect weakens and endangers the friendship.

Lama Tsongkhapa suggested that instead of jealousy we try to cultivate the habit of extracting joy from the good things we see in others. He commented that by rejoicing in a good quality or situation that we perceive in others, we share in the joy of having it ourselves. We may not own the mountain, but we are able to walk freely on it without impediment. For example, others may play a musical instrument better than we do; if we just rejoice in this fact rather than be jealous of it, then when we listen to them play we enjoy their music fully, whereas if we are infused with jealousy, every note they play irritates.

7

What enemies of the state are
destroying our happiness and prosperity?
All the various emotional afflictions
that disturb the threads of thought.

Here the Seventh Dalai Lama calls the afflicted emotions "enemies of the state," likening the elements of a human being to
those of a nation. For this he draws his inspiration from the
eleventh-century Indian master Naropa, who in turn had used a
passage from one of Buddha's abhidharma teachings, in which a
living person and his or her aggregates are compared to a city-
state.

In this metaphor, each of us is king or queen of our own
little kingdom. We all have an aspect of our being which serves
as our minister of external affairs, another as minister of health,
another as minister of finance, another as minister of defense,
and so forth. When the person's mind is clear and lucid, each of
these ministers serves us well; but when the mind is overpowered by afflicted emotions, our private little nation is thrown
into chaos. We create actions of body, speech and mind that bring
us problems in our relationships, health, careers, and even personal safety.

The afflicted emotions "disturb the threads of thought." Living the moments of our life is like weaving a tapestry. To create
a tapestry we need a steady hand. The word "disturb" here could
alternatively be translated as "shake." We cannot work well with
a shaking hand, just as we cannot live happily when the mind is
shaking with disturbed emotions.

8

What is the prison difficult to escape,
even though we hold the keys?
Entangled personal relationships,
such as attachments to family and friends.

Relationships with others should be based on qualities like respect, dignity and trust. When personal attachments enter into
the equation, everything goes wrong. Affection and freedom are
replaced by obsession and manipulation.

We see this clearly, for example, in the relationship between
parents and children. When parents replace openness and trust
with clinging and attachment, the result is resentment and bit-
terness in the child. The natural affection becomes twisted into
a force of domination.

Similarly, when two people in love allow their affection to be
usurped by attachment, both end up feeling entrapped and controlled by the other. The loved one, rather than being appreciated, comes to be viewed with enmity.

As the twelfth-century Tibetan yogi Milarepa put it, "In the
beginning the loved one seems like a divine being. But when
attachment rules, soon he or she seems like a demon. And in the
end the formerly loved one seems like a prison guard, with oneself as the prisoner."

9

What are the chains which bind one
even when one has left that prison?
Attachment to worldly activities
even when living in retreat.

The First Dalai Lama once said, "It is easy to change one's outer
circumstances, but hard to change the samsaric mind." In other
words, we can easily generate a strong spiritual determination,
and by means of that inspired resolve can take up the practice
of meditation; but it is not so easy to leave behind our habitual
ways of thinking. He concluded his remark by saying, "However, although the mind is slow to improve, with persistent efforts in the threefold sphere of learning, contemplation and meditation, even the most dull person can attain exalted states of
consciousness."

Once the young Fifth Dalai Lama was in meditation retreat
in the Potala. A clairvoyant lama friend of his came to visit him
one day, but was turned away by his attendant on the grounds
that the retreat was still not completed. "Well," the lama re-
torted, "tell him that I saw him in the central market earlier this
morning."

Later when the attendant took the Fifth Dalai Lama his food
he related the story to him. The Great Fifth laughed and replied, "Indeed, during my morning session my mind wandered
away from the object of meditation, and I found myself day-
dreaming about walking around in the market."

10

What demon possesses one
and repays friendship with pain?
Misleading friends, who only increase
one's negative karma and delusions.

In one of his works on methods to transform the mind the Seventh Dalai Lama wrote, "A wind blowing over a sandalwood forest smells sweet, but blowing over shit it smells foul. Likewise, whether your companions are positive or negative, your lifestyle is affected accordingly. Therefore it is important to choose wisely."

Buddhism advocates cultivating tolerance and compassion for all living beings; but when one is still on initial levels of training it is important to maintain a spiritually conducive environment. This is especially true when it comes to choosing the people with whom one shares one's time.

Lama Tsongkhapa wrote, "Life is short and precious. Therefore be kind to all living beings, but choose your friends wisely. Remember that bad habits are easily acquired and then hard to lose, whereas positive habits are acquired only with much effort and discipline, but are easily lost to mindlessness."

11

Who are the slippery monsters
that slide between love and hate?
False friends and those around us
who only pretend to wish us well.

Worldly people look for ego-reinforcement in the friends and associates that they choose. The link is based on vanity and brings no happiness, peace, prosperity or spiritual benefit.

Kachen Yeshey Gyaltsen, the guru of the Eighth Dalai Lama, was a monk from the remote areas of the Mount Everest region. He did a twelve-year meditation retreat in a cave hermitage near Mt. Everest and then returned to Kyirong, the nearby valley of his birth. No one showed any real interest in him, and he lived in relative obscurity.

Then one day he was invited to Lhasa and asked to be the guru of the young Eighth Dalai Lama. This exalted position instantly transformed him from obscurity into one of the most highly respected lamas in the country. The people of his valley immediately began to take note.

One day a group of them showed up in Lhasa and asked for an audience with him. He arranged a big banquet for them, and the food was brought in. On his own plate, however, there was only money and jewels. He looked at and then prostrated to it, remarking, "Previously when I lived as a simple monk and meditator, nobody showed any interest in me. It seemed that I had no friends and no relatives. Now that I have come to a position of prestige I suddenly have an abundance of both. I bow to wealth and fame, that gave me friends and relatives where previously I had none."

The Seventh Dalai Lama likens false friends to "slippery monsters that slide between love and hate," for they are fair weather
friends that come when times are good but turn away at the
slightest provocation. Their interests are not in real friendship,
but in gaining something by association.

12

Who is the drunken fool
always bringing suffering onto himself?
The one who spends his time lusting
after comfort, pleasure, wealth and fame.

Everyone wants happiness, and nobody wants suffering. This is
true with all forms of life, from the smallest insect to the biggest human.

However, the effectiveness of our quest for happiness comes
from the spheres within which we conduct our search. Happiness which relies upon external conditions will always remain
unstable, for external phenomena are constantly in a state of
flux. In brief, the only stable happiness is that which is produced
within the mind itself and is based on spiritual knowledge.

The above verse by the Seventh Dalai Lama refers to what is
known in Buddhism as the eight worldly concerns: pleasure and
pain, gain and loss, praise and criticism, and finally, fame and
infamy. Ordinary human beings concern themselves almost exclusively with these eight, chasing the positive four and run-
ning away from the negative four. This is reasonable enough
when done with an understanding that life brings both positive
and negative, that some of both is inevitable, and that one can
learn and benefit from both. However, when one expects only
the positive and fears the negative, one's inner peace and happiness will always remain unstable.

One should follow the advice of the twelfth-century Tibetan
mystic Milarepa, who said, "Turn your back on the eight worldly
concerns and meditate on the unfulfilling nature of the ordinary. Direct the mind instead to the spiritual path. All fears are
transcended and inner happiness is attained."

13

What is the weight that brings down
the painful bubble of misery?
Any clinging one has
to superficial, transient affairs.

Situations, like people, are always in a state of flux. When one
bases one's inner peace and happiness on the presence of a particular situation, one is setting oneself up for a fall. Here the
Seventh Dalai Lama likens clinging to a weight tied to one's
back. No matter how high one is, it brings one down a notch or
two, and in the end produces unhappiness.

Lama Tsongkhapa wrote, "We are born alone, we die alone,
and we travel alone into the hereafter. During the brief period
between birth and death we should maintain a sense of this
aloneness. When we depend on external people and situations
for our strength and happiness, how can we ever expect stable
happiness? The only reliable friend is spiritual knowledge; the
only truly helpful possession is one's own inner character."

Also elsewhere the Seventh Dalai Lama wrote, "Fantasies
about material objects and the winds of the eight worldly concerns are completely misleading. Because of clinging to things
which give only temporary fulfillment, at death one is weighed
down with the pain of an empty soul."

14

Who is the trickster stealing from others
while living in a remote hermitage?
The person in retreat supported by others
who spends his time in vain.

It was the custom in Tibet, as well as in other traditional Buddhist countries of Asia, for those who entered a meditation hermitage to receive the support of family, friends or other patrons.
People not in retreat were generally happy to support retreaters,
on the belief that in this way they would share in the spiritual
energy of the meditation practice. In more remote hermitages
the food was supplied by the head lama of the center, which he
generally paid for by undertaking teaching tours.

In either case, to accept this support and yet not make pure
effort to accomplish the practice was considered to be a deed
karmically equal to stealing from a temple.

In another of his texts the Seventh Dalai Lama wrote, "One
may shave one's head and put on a hundred sets of beautiful
robes, yet one is still carried away into misery if one lives un-
wisely and is overpowered by attachment. O you lazy mind, why
don't you get the message!"

In traditional Tibetan society, one in four Tibetans became a
monk or nun for at least the first third of their life, and others
became a monastic for the last third. In addition, many of the
ordinary laypeople undertook occasional meditation retreats for
periods from a few months to several years. The Tibetans regarded the spiritual energy generated by this unique activity to
be a subliminal contribution to world peace and prosperity. With
the support that the portion of the population in retreat received,
however, came a great responsibility. To abuse the tradition in

order to avoid work or social responsibility was considered a strong negative karma that would bring unhappiness in this life and lower rebirth in the hereafter. As the Seventh Dalai Lama puts it, such a person is a "trickster stealing from others while living in a remote hermitage."

15

Who is the hollow exhibitionist resembling
a child wearing the ornaments of a god?
The performer of tantric rituals
who is without the inner yogas.

Tantric Buddhism is rich in shamanic ritual. Healings, exorcisms, rain-making rites, and rituals for increasing fertility, attracting wealth, and warding off obstacles are just a few of the types of activities that a tantric monk or shaman may be requested to perform. In addition to these there are many types of tantric meditation that are performed by the monastic clergy as liturgy for communal temple practice, such as self-initiations, invocations of mandala deities and Dharma protectors, and so forth.

In many of these ceremonies the ritualist dresses in a special tantric costume associated with the specific practice being performed. Any traveller in a Tibetan Buddhist region may witness numerous events of this nature.

Before engaging in such rituals, however, the tantric practitioner should first undertake the standard retreats in order to accomplish the inner yogas that bestow power over the subtle energies of body and mind. This was the tradition established by the great Indian adepts and brought to the Land of Snows by the early Tibetan masters.

The First Dalai Lama once wrote, "To present oneself as a tantric yogi without first going into the mountains and accomplishing the tantric yogas is like a fox pretending to be a lion."

16

What is the load heavy to carry,
difficult to put down, and always harmful?
One's own samsaric aggregates,
that are conditioned by karma and delusion.

Buddhism speaks of the self as being a mere sense of "I" imputed upon the aggregates, or facets, of body and mind. The Sanskrit word for aggregate is *skandha*, which means something like a collection, or compound, of factors. My "I," or self, is my sense of individuality as formed from and conditioned by the factors or aggregates that make up my life.

With ordinary people, the aggregates of being are conditioned by karma and klesha, or, respectively, predispositions of behavior and distorted mental/emotional states. Because these are a mixture of positive and negative forces, the person alternately experiences happiness and suffering. However, as a person grows in the wisdom of enlightenment, the karmic forces and distorted mental/emotional states are purified, with the result that happiness becomes stronger and suffering less frequent. Eventually enlightenment is achieved, and with it comes eternal and all-pervasive happiness.

The Seventh Dalai Lama here describes the skandhas as being "contaminated," for the relationship between the "I" and the skandhas is tainted by misidentification. That is to say, we tend to think of the I as being a concrete phenomenon that somehow is truly existent either together with the aggregates or separate from them. When we mis-identify the I in this way, karma and klesha hold great strength over us, causing the skandhas to arise in various modes of unpleasantness and suffering.

This is the load to be put down in the quest for enlightenment.

17

W̶ho is it that everyone mistrusts
and is laughed at by all the world?
The person who constantly lies
and attempts to deceive others.

With the previous verses the Seventh Dalai Lama addresses many
of the spiritual problems that afflict the mind. He now turns to
how these inner distortions lead to external expression, thus
bringing unhappiness to self and others.

He begins by addressing what are known as the four negative
karmas of speech: lying, harsh speech, slander and idle gossip.

The first of these, lying, he links to deception. As he puts it,
the person "who constantly lies and lives other than he speaks"
is an object of mistrust and is "ridiculed by all the world."

In Buddhism, speech is considered a sacred ability. Humans
have a heightened ability of thought and articulation, and with
this comes a sacred trust. It is one of the primary factors distin-
guishing humans from more primitive life forms, and is a source
of great power for us. Through speech we transmit knowledge
from generation to generation, and even pass on the keys to
higher wisdom and enlightenment. Both conventional culture
and spiritual knowledge rely upon it as a fundamental tool. To
use the extraordinary facility of communication in order to mis-
lead and deceive others is, as one twelfth-century Tibetan mystic put it, "turning a god into a malicious spirit."

18

What sharp weapons slice hearts
when people meet with each other?
The saying of harsh and cruel things,
and the criticizing of others' faults.

Here the Seventh Dalai Lama introduces the second and third
negative karmas created by means of speech: harsh words and
slander.

He calls these "sharp weapons that slice hearts," for our words
are instruments that cut others deeply when we use them harm-
fully. They are most commonly used on, and also most hurtful
to, those we love and with whom we are most close. In many
ways abusive speech is a more profound form of harming others
than is physical violence, for its impact goes deeper.

Both of these negative karmas of speech have as their underlying force the thought to harm. Unfortunately in this age
of darkness both are also considered normal and acceptable.
Those following the enlightenment tradition, however, always
try to speak gently and with the desire to be helpful and meaningful.

Slander does not only refer to speaking untruthfully in such
a way as will create division between others. It also includes the
expression of irrelevant facts or truths while holding an inner
intent to create divisions between others.

19

What invisible wind brings weakness
and wanders without end?
Indulgence in babble and chatter
devoid of any meaning.

Meaningless babble is the fourth negative karma created by means of speech. Of the ten negative karmas—three physical, four vocal, and three mental—idle gossip is described as being the least severe but most frequent of them all, and also the most common with humans. It is the greatest time-waster. As the Seventh Dalai Lama puts it, this unwholesome karma "brings weakness and wanders without end."

The human ability to articulate and communicate is a primary key to our success and happiness as a species. Therefore Lama Tsongkhapa once said, "The person following the path of higher being and enlightenment resolves to speak truthfully, gently, helpfully, and meaningfully." With this simple statement he pointed out how to avoid the four negative karmas of speech and instead cultivate the four positive ones.

The great lama Sakya Pandita said, "When you have nothing meaningful to say, simply enjoy the silence. If you cannot keep your tongue from flapping, tie a piece of string around it. For some that is the only remedy."

20

What evil spirits devour others
even when they are not hungry?
People in power who abuse those under
    them,
and consider them as worthless as grass.

The Seventh Dalai Lama was invested with the role of being both spiritual and temporal leader of the Tibetan people. He was also the highest incarnate lama in the Gelukpa school, which had a vast following not only in Tibet, but also in the Mongol nations, the Himalayan kingdoms of the Indian sub-continent, as well as various regions of China. He was especially popular with the Manchu rulers, who at the time held sway over all of China.

As such, he was very much aware of the dangers of worldly power, and of how a corrupt and cruel leader could bring great suffering to people. Tibet was a federation of several hundred kingdoms and nomadic tribes, each of which had its own internal system of semi-autonomous self-government. His duty as spiritual and temporal head of the nation was to inspire the local kings and chieftains to honor the enlightenment code of ethics in their rule, and to see themselves as serving rather than ruling.

His role was not like that of a European pope, however, for Buddhism has no ex-communication, and there is no real centralization of authority. For example, every monk or nun is responsible for his or her own moral purity, and there is no institution for forcing an impure monastic to disrobe. Every monastery sets its own standards in this regard, and although a monastery can expel a monk or nun from their premises, it cannot take their robes from them.

This verse is directed not only to kings and chieftains, but to all in positions of authority, from government officials to heads of humble households.

21

Who lives in the hell realms
while appearing in the world of human
 beings?
The person who works and toils
under a corrupt executive or boss.

In the previous verse the Seventh Dalai Lama points out the responsibilities of someone in a position of leadership and power, and the difficulties for others when this position is abused. Now he turns to the situation of those in positions of service or employment. As he puts it, when we allow ourselves to remain in the employ of "a corrupt executive or boss," we allow ourselves to descend into the hell realms.

This is true in two main ways. In terms of our immediate experience, we never know peace and happiness when we allow ourselves to follow the direction of a corrupt boss. The corrupt boss pushes us in negative and unpleasant ways, disturbing our peace of mind and often even physically endangering us. The negative character of the master negatively impacts on the worker.

Secondly, in terms of a longer perspective, when we live under a corrupt boss we will have to engage in corruption ourselves, and thus enter into the ways by which negative karma is accumulated. This in turn will produce lower rebirth in the life to follow.

In the above verse the Seventh Dalai Lama is referring mainly to the first of these two effects.

22

W̲hat hungry ghosts suffer with deprivation
while having food, wealth and possessions?
Wealthy people who are so bound by
    miserliness
that they cannot enjoy their own wealth.

Buddhism speaks of the world of reincarnation as being formed
of six realms, three of which are called "the three unhappy
realms" and the other three "the three happy realms." The three
unhappy ones, also known as the three lower realms, are those
of the hell beings, the hungry ghosts and the animal world.
Through anger and cruelty we take rebirth in the first of these;
through attachment and craving we take rebirth in the second;
and through unmindful actions and instinctual behavior we take
rebirth in the third. All three realms are also metaphors for human states, the ghost realm being a metaphor for the mind-state
of craving and attachment.

The Seventh Dalai Lama says that wealthy people "who are
so bound by miserliness that they cannot enjoy their own wealth"
are like hungry ghosts. In Tibetan iconography this type of
ghost is depicted as having a belly as big as a mountain but a
throat no larger than a barley straw. The image is one of per-
petual craving, wherein satiation is never known.

Buddhism has no problems with worldly success, nor even
worldly indulgence. Many kings and wealthy businessmen have
achieved enlightenment. The problem comes when this success
just enhances ego-grasping rather than enriching the spirit of
the person and enhancing the role of friend to the world. Worldly
possessions are like a hammer; used as a tool, they can contribute
to the happiness of self and others; used as a weapon, they bring
harm.

23

Who pretends to be a human being
but in fact is but a beast?
The person lost in unknowing
and with no interest in spiritual excellence.

The Seventh Dalai Lama dedicates the above three verses to the
three lower realms of rebirth—hells, ghost realms and animal
world. In particular, these verses reveal how the three lower
realms find their way into the life of a human being. We descend into the hells when we accept wrong livelihood; we become like a ghost when we live in greed and attachment; and we
are no better than a beast when we abandon the quest for spiritual excellence.

The Second Dalai Lama wrote to one of his disciples, "O
Jampal Drakpa, this human body with the freedoms and endowments is a supreme vessel for spiritual training. Think over the
precious opportunity that is yours. Take advantage of it. You
may strive for all of eternity at worldly works, but you will never
see an end to them. Jampal Drakpa, do not leave yourself armed
only with regret when the Lord of Death strikes."

Also the Third Dalai Lama wrote, "By means of relying upon
a spiritual master and working with the laws of cause and effect
you can take advantage of this extremely valuable human birth,
a life-form hard to find and of tremendous potential, a treasure
more precious than a wish-fulfilling gem. Therefore apply yourself to the task of the spiritual quest, and do not let this most
rare opportunity slip away."

24

Who is troubled with a noisy mind
even though living in a quiet place?
The one dwelling in solitary retreat
who engages in ways unbecoming to the
    wise.

The biggest obstacle to spiritual knowledge is the restless and
roaming mind that flips from object to object without ever set-
tling into anything in any depth.

One undertakes meditation retreat in order to quiet the mind
and bring it into clear focus, so that it can penetrate deeply into
spiritually significant realities such as impermanence, the emptiness nature of self and phenomena, love and compassion and
so forth. However, if the meditator does not follow the disciplines concomitant with retreat, but instead just indulges in laziness and distraction, the retreat is of no value. A successful
retreat leads the mind in the direction of the attainment of
samadhi, or higher meditative power.

Many Tibetans would do the three-year retreat associated
with the mandala practices of the tantric system into which they
were initiated. Several schools of Tibetan Buddhism even
awarded the title of "lama" or "master teacher" to anyone com-
pleting this retreat. Here the Seventh Dalai Lama warns that
merely placing oneself in a retreat environment does not neces-
sarily produce the desired effects. Many young Tibetans would
undertake this retreat solely in order to acquire the title of lama,
but while in retreat would idle away their time, anxiously awaiting the completion of the time period so that they could emerge
and receive the respect and prestige associated with the title.

25

What is the negative omen indicating
the advent of many misfortunes?
The exaggeration of beneficial qualities
in the objects that appear to the senses.

The objects that appear to the five senses can benefit us in natural ways, but when we exaggerate their value they easily instead bring us harm.

For example, tasty food is healthy to the body, and a healthy body encourages a healthy and clear mind. However, when we exaggerate the importance of the tastiness of food we miss the essential point of the function of food, which is to sustain the health and well-being of the body. We end up living on chocolate eclairs and soda pop. This is not healthy for either the body or the mind. Therefore Nagarjuna said, "Regard the food that you eat as medicine."

Similarly with the objects of the other four senses, each has its naturally beneficial mode of being. However, when we exaggerate any element within them we suffer from an according distortion. Attachment to specific pretty sights causes us to be unhappy when these are not present, and to miss out on the natural beauty of whatever is present. The same goes for scents, sounds and sensations. A conceptual orientation toward one brand of any of them causes unhappiness and discomfort in the mind whenever this is absent, and also causes us to miss out on the natural appropriateness of what is present in the moment.

In Tantric Buddhism the practitioner adopts the discipline of taking whatever objects arise in the field of the senses as expressions of the natural play of primordial bliss and wisdom.

In other words, an emphasis is placed on the natural perfection of whatever arises. This allows one to take every sensory experience as beautiful, and thus by-pass the prejudices that distort and obscure the immediacy of being.

As the Second Dalai Lama put it, "When one has eliminated the prejudices of this over that, the natural perfection of the moment automatically becomes clear."

26

What is the strong and deadly poison
that, although small, brings great pain?
Small acts of negative karma done
without regret or application of the
    antidotes.

Success in life is not so much a matter of taking care of the big
things, but rather of paying attention to the details. When we
take care of the details, the bigger issues are naturally handled
successfully.

Very few people have problems with major acts of negative
karma. These rarely arise. However, small acts of negative karma
can occur hundreds of times a day when we do not watch out
for them. For example, not many of us engage in killing, but we
often speak harshly to our loved ones, or allow the mind to en-
tertain thoughts based on attachment or aversion. This is what
the Seventh Dalai Lama means by "small acts of negative karma."

He adds, "done without regret or application of the antidotes." Spiritual progress comes from refining our life on a day-
by-day basis. Buddha recommended that before we go to sleep
at night we sit quietly in meditation and re-live our day, tallying
up what was done successfully and what unsuccessfully. We
should rejoice in the positive and purify the negative by means
of the four opponent forces, or four antidotes.

The first of the four antidotes is regret. Without this, there
is no hope of counteracting the behavioral pattern. The second
is the resolve to eliminate the behavioral pattern from within
one's repertoire of acceptable activity. The third is the strength-
ening of the foundation, which means invoking the spiritual

forces within oneself and generating universal love and compassion. The fourth is the application of a purification technique, such as mantra, visualization, and so forth. After these four have been applied one should generate the sense that the negative energy has been completely washed away and the syndrome has been utterly transcended.

27

What is the ball of dirt
that can stain even a god?
Not guarding with close attention
the spiritual precepts one has taken.

The Buddha gave three basic levels of spiritual application, known in Sanskrit as Hinayana, Mahayana and Vajrayana, or Way of Individual Liberation, Way of Universal Concern and the Tantric Way. Most Tibetans practice these three "Ways" in a sequential order. They begin with the first level by cultivating greater personal freedom through application of the methods that reduce the mental activities of attachment, aversion and ignorance. They cultivate the second level by generating universal love and compassion through meditating on all living beings as having been one's own mother, father and loved one in a previous life. Finally, they cultivate the third level by meditating on the self as being a tantric mandala deity, or buddha-form, and the world as being a pure expression of primordial bliss and wisdom in the form of a mandala.

Each of these three levels has its own specific precepts or disciplines, and success in the practice depends upon maintaining these with care. Indian and Tibetan literature provides long lists of these, but they all boil down to quintessential principles. The essence of the discipline on the first level is always to avoid any expression of body, speech or mind that is harmful to others. The essential discipline on the second level is to always hold only love and compassion for others, directed by the aspiration to achieve enlightenment as a means of benefiting the world, and supported by the practice of the six perfections. Finally, the essence of the precepts associated with the Tantric Way is to always see oneself and others as blissful mandala deities, and the world as a pure expression of primordial bliss and wisdom.

The words "a ball of dirt that can stain even a god" suggest tantric practice, wherein one sees oneself and others as mandala deities. The Seventh Dalai Lama's point is that even a high tantric practitioner should respect the three levels of precepts. He makes this emphasis because in his time many Tibetan lamas used their tantric practice as an excuse for indulgence and slovenliness.

28

What is the body odor
easy to acquire but hard to lose?
Habits picked up from people
whose lives are far from spiritual ways.

Buddhism regards the human world as a training ground for
the enlightenment process. Living beings take rebirth here in
order to learn and evolve. The conditions of the human environment change with the millennia in order to suit the needs of
the trainees. Those riding the winds of positive karma are born
as humans in a particular time and place in order to meet with
those conditions most appropriate to their needs.

The present era is called *kaliyuga*, or "the dark age," for in it
we are confronted by five harsh conditions: life-force is weak;
delusions and afflicted emotions predominate everywhere; the
times are violent; the living beings presently incarnate are mostly
of low character; and false ideas and attitudes are mistaken for
truth. As a result, human civilization is filled with social struc-
tures, philosophical attitudes and behavioral norms that are in
direct contradiction to and obstructive of spiritual growth.

On the positive side, the smallest point of light is clearly
visible simply because everything is so dark, just as a candle
flame in the daylight is almost invisible but at night is clearly
seen from a great distance. Similarly, those born in the kaliyuga
who enter into the path of spiritual knowledge quickly achieve
their goals, for the steps on the path are easily distinguished.

The biggest obstacle to enlightenment in the kaliyuga is the
temptation to follow the norms of society, for society is mostly
on the wrong track. Therefore when the eleventh-century

Kadampa master Lama Drom Tonpa was once asked how best to follow the path of spiritual knowledge he replied, "The masses have their heads on backwards. If you want to get things right, first look at how they think and behave, and consider going the opposite way."

29

What is the sharp thorn
quick to pierce but hard to extract?
Vulgar and insensitive ways
that negatively impact the minds of others.

Just as we ourselves easily acquire negative habits of thinking, speaking and behaving through our contact with others, so too do our actions of body, speech and mind create an effect upon others. The Buddha gave the simile of a small stone thrown into a pool; everything we do sets off a wave pattern that spreads slowly into all directions. Whenever we harm or insult another, that person carries a karmic tension in the mind which waits for an object on which to unleash itself.

Especially, those of us who have set out on a spiritual path have a greater responsibility. The Fifth Dalai Lama said that we should regard ourselves as ambassadors of the enlightened beings, and should strive to bring spiritual dignity, compassion and wisdom into every movement of body, speech and mind. Then we become like a candle from which the light of peace and happiness passes to all other candles with which it comes into contact. Otherwise, we continue to be part of the problem rather than part of the solution and to spread problematic energy rather than healing energy.

The Thirteenth Dalai Lama said, "We can be good to someone a hundred times, but if we insult or harm them just once, they quickly forget the hundred kindnesses and remember that one slight for a long time. Therefore always be mindful in your exchanges with others."

30

Who is the navigator leading us
to the various realms of suffering?
The power of karma and delusion,
that bring us into the lower realms.

Buddha's first teaching after his enlightenment was that concerning the four noble truths: suffering, its causes, liberation,
and the path to liberation.

These are listed here *not* in the order in which they occur,
but rather in the order in which they are perceived. That is to
say, firstly we observe a suffering, and then we search for its
cause. Similarly, firstly we understand the principle of spiritual
liberation, and then we search for a path that will give rise to it.

The order in which the four unfold is different. Here firstly
we create a cause of suffering, and sometime later we experience the results of that cause; and firstly we cultivate the path
to liberation, and as a result of our application we experience
liberation. Buddha gave the example of a farmer who reaps the
seeds that he sows.

The causes of all suffering are twofold: karma and klesha.
Karma literally means "action," but the sense is that every time
we think, say or do something we create a memory imprint on
the mind. This imprint has a resonance that accords with the
nature of the act, and in turn sends out an energy field that
fosters an unfolding result. In brief, negative karmic imprints
bring suffering and positive ones bring happiness.

As we saw earlier in verses four to nine, *klesha* refers to distorted spiritual and/or emotional states of mind. These are en-
couraged by the negative karmic imprints, and also facilitate the
unfolding of further negative karmic imprints, in the sense that

a habit quickly brings more of the same. In brief, when no active negative karmic energy nor klesha are present, no causes of suffering are experienced.

31

W̲hat is the invisible disease
that pains us day and night?
The disease of continually aging
and watching health and youth fade.

The key to entering into true spiritual experience is an understanding of the frustrating nature of unenlightened existence.
This is illustrated by the way in which Buddha himself as a
young man was moved to abandon the ordinary in search of the
transcendental. He was a young warrior prince living in the lap
of luxury, insulated against the horrors of ugliness. Then by
chance on an outing from the palace he saw firstly a sick man,
then an old man, and next a corpse. All three were twisted and
disfigured by the signs of suffering and unhappiness. These three
experiences greatly disturbed his mind. Finally he saw an old
sage sitting deeply in meditation, his countenance radiating peace
and happiness.

Ａs a result of witnessing these four signs he resolved to go
the way of the sage, and shortly thereafter left the palace in
search of spiritual knowledge. His search led him to many teachers and to experiment with many spiritual methods, until eventually he achieved enlightenment. He taught widely for the next
forty-five years, and then passed away from within the sphere
of spiritual ecstasy.

Ordinary people cling to the body, and their happiness depends upon bodily vigor. As life slips by and old age sets in,
their inner vibrancy and joy also fade. In the end they die weak
and in despair.

Alternatively the sage who has achieved knowledge ages with beauty and grace, for he or she has touched to the heart of the immortal wisdom, identifying with it rather than with the ever-deteriorating physical base that is the body. He/she sees the body as a precious vessel able to carry the mind to wisdom, and not as a mere instrument of mundane experience.

32

Who is the master executioner
slaughtering all sentient beings?
The terrifying Lord of Death,
who has power over the entire world.

The entrance chamber of most Tibetan temples is decorated with a painting known as "the wheel of life." This image depicts a ferocious figure, the Lord of Death, holding a globe in his mouth. Inside the globe are illustrations of the six realms of ordinary rebirth, with its six types of living beings—hell denizens, ghosts, animals, humans, titans and gods. The symbolism is that all living beings, from the lowest hell denizen to the highest god, are prey to the laws of impermanence, aging and death. All six realms are but ephemeral states of being, and when the karmic force that brought one into them has exhausted itself one dies and reincarnates elsewhere. The painting usually includes the figure of a buddha or bodhisattva standing off to the side, one hand pointing upward, to symbolize the path of spiritual awakening by which ordinary reincarnation is transcended.

The First Dalai Lama wrote, "Many are the steps we take in this life, and we always carry sacred nature deep within. Yet rarely do we take note of it when we allow the negative mind to arise. Make your priority the nectars of immortality, the wisdom that appreciates the world and beyond."

In other words, the force through which we transcend death is wisdom itself. And of course even wisdom only eliminates death in terms of the ordinary experience of reincarnation. The wise also age and die; they just do so in a more sublime manner.

33

Who suffer most deeply
of all the beings in the world?
Those with no self-discipline
who are overpowered by delusion.

Generally speaking a person is always in one of two types of
mind states: *shen-wang*, or "other-powered" and *rang-wang*, or
"self-powered." The former refers to the times when we do not
keep the mind in positive spheres, and consequently are driven
by distorted emotional or cognitive states; the latter refers to
when we keep the mind focussed through the application of spiritual methods.

It could also be said that there are two types of living beings: those who are directed mainly by negative mind states,
and thus are mainly "other-powered," and those who are directed
mainly by spiritual forces, and thus are mainly "self-powered."
The second of the two have eliminated the coarse delusions and
afflicted emotions, and have aroused the innate seeds of wisdom. Thus they hold the reins of their destiny in their own
hands.

Distorted mind states and afflicted emotions are the principal inner agents giving rise to external courses of action that
create unhappiness for self and others. Due to anger, attachment, jealousy, prejudiced attitudes and so forth we misjudge
the dynamics of the moment and mistake the flow of energies
that constitute the transformations of body, speech and mind.

The remedy is the taming of the negative mind and the
arousal of wisdom. However, these goals are not easily or quickly
accomplished. Therefore those who have taken up the enlightenment path rely upon self-discipline. We cannot always have

the wisdom to be free of anger, but through the will-power of self-discipline we can refrain from acts based on anger. Similarly, we may not yet have the wisdom that is free from prejudices, but we can discipline ourselves to mind our own business.

Undeveloped beings are almost always in a state of *shen-wang*. The more developed we become, the less time we spend in *shen-wang* states, and the more time in *rang-wang*, until eventually we achieve the transcendental wisdom that keeps us eternally in *rang-wang*.

34

Who are the most evil
of all beings in the world?
Those who use their strength and power
as a means of harming others

We tend to think of power as a problem only of the rich and mighty, but in fact we all have it to some degree, even if only over our children and family members, or over the animals and insects with which we share our environment. No matter what the degree of power we have, our responsibility is to use it wisely. In brief, it should be harnessed to the increase of the good and the wholesome, and used as a means of contributing to happiness for self and others.

Buddhism states that the conditions of this life that provide us with strength and power come to us as a result of positive karma. We gained these conditions through past efforts and auspicious deeds. Now that we have the fruits of our work we should take care how we utilize them, for they in turn are the seeds of a future harvest. We can create a positive snowball effect by intensifying the positive energy that has been set in motion, or we can twist it and cause the energy to turn back on itself, thus reversing the momentum. As one twelfth-century Kadampa lama put it, when we misuse our positive inner or outer conditions, we "take a blessing and make it into a curse."

Lama Tsongkhapa once commented that when people of low character gain power they become arrogant and harmful, whereas when those of high character gain it their humility and sense of universal responsibility just increase. We should follow the example of the latter.

35

Who is the biggest loser
of all beings in the world?
He who lives falsely
and in contradiction to karmic law.

The Tibetan word for "karmic law" is *ley gyu drey*, which literally means "cause-effect activity."

As the Second Dalai Lama puts it, "All things have the great
void as their ultimate nature; nothing has any separate, true or
inherently findable existence. Yet on the conventional level of
reality things appear to the mind, and function in accordance
with the karmic laws of cause and effect."

Karmic law operates on both immediate and long-term levels. That is to say, the actions that we do through body, speech
and mind have an immediate impact upon this life we lead, an
impact that we experience materially, psychologically, socially,
financially and so forth. However, they go beyond that, leaving
seeds of memory on the mind that eventually become instincts
and conditioning factors. These are carried on the mental continuum into the hereafter, where they act as the driving force of
the mind and influence how we evolve and take rebirth, and the
mental and physical conditions that will prevail in that rebirth.
This continues until enlightenment, when the forces of karma
and delusion are utterly and forever transcended.

The early Kadampa lamas said, "Of all things that can be
known, the most important is the cause-effect nature of activity.
This is the key to success in all other spheres."

36

Who willingly makes himself into a slave
owned by everyone in the world?
The feeble-minded person
who has no self-confidence.

The Great Way taught by the Buddha advocates altruism and universal love for others. One is instructed to meditate on all living beings as having been a mother, father, brother and sister to one in many past lives, and to make one's every action into a source of happiness and fulfillment for them. As the Second Dalai Lama put it, "One should try in every way to avoid harming others, and instead always be of benefit to them."

This is the Way of the Bodhisattva, the Enlightenment Hero/ Heroine, and therefore must be practiced in accordance with the six perfections: generosity, discipline, patience, joyous effort, meditation and wisdom. To carry the weight of these six wheels one must be strong of heart, endowed with unwavering courage and inspired by profound self-confidence. Without the six perfections, any work for the benefit of others is, as Lama Tsongkhapa put it, "punching at the sky." Nothing of value is accomplished.

All schools of Tibetan Buddhism begin their trainings by introducing the practitioner to the meditations on the nature of the precious human incarnation, with its eight freedoms and ten endowments, and its capacity to achieve final enlightenment. The aim of this step is to instill the trainee with appreciation for his or her own infinite capacity, and thus arouse the mind of strong self-confidence. The eight freedoms refer to being born in a time and place that is free from conditions in which spiritual practice is difficult or impossible; the ten endowments refer to being born in a time and place where an enlightenment tradition exists, and having the inner predispositions to engage in a spiritual path.

Buddha said, "You are your own savior. Who else can save you?" We live in a gregarious world, and unless we learn to take responsibility for our own situation, our life will always be a mere response to the conditions that prevail around us. The birth of true self-confidence marks the beginning of real success, for from that moment on we become navigators of our own ship, rather than merely being blown wherever the winds of society randomly push us.

37

Who is most ridiculed
by the people of the world?
Those who, when they lose their worldly
    position,
also lose their spiritual perspective.

When the Buddha taught the four noble truths—suffering, its causes, liberation and the path—or four realities as seen by the *aryas*—those who have direct realization of the true nature of reality—he spoke of the path to liberation as being comprised of the eightfold path walked by the aryas: right vision, right understanding, right speech, right action, right livelihood, right aspiration, right mindfulness and right samadhi.

Our worldly position should be regarded as our practice of right livelihood, i.e., as a career through which we contribute materially to the well-being of self and others. For some people this will mean considerable wealth, power and prestige. However, outer circumstances are always unstable. Kings can be reduced to prisoners or even slaves by changing political conditions; the wealthy can be reduced to beggars. Events like these have occurred many times in the course of history.

For someone firmly based in the eightfold path, however, such external changes are not seen as catastrophic. Having meditated on impermanence, the unstable nature of samsara, and so forth, that person faces decline in worldly status with strength and courage. Moreover, worldly position is but one of the eightfold limbs of the path, and the power of the other seven allows any change in livelihood to be taken with grace, calm and dignity.

The wise person sees his or her livelihood merely as an external theater, and plays the role in order to benefit self and others. When the theater changes and another role is required, he or she plays it with equal dedication, warmth and humor.

38

Who is but a skilled merchant
among beings of the world?
The patron who gives charity
hoping to get a return.

Most spiritual traditions of the world advocate the practice of
generosity. As Jesus put it, "It is better to give than to receive."
(Try begging for a day, and then practicing generosity for a day,
and see which of the two you prefer.)

However, an act of generosity is only spiritual when it is
performed with a pure heart. That is to say, its aim should be to
benefit the recipient; it should not be used as a manipulative tool
to benefit oneself.

To give in order to get something in return, such as public
recognition or the affections of the recipient, is merely an in-
vestment in one's own worldly concerns, and is of no spiritual
value whatsoever. It is no different than buying stocks and bonds,
or putting money into some business or other. To do so is not
harmful, but also is not spiritually significant.

This is on the conventional level. On the ultimate level generosity only becomes a spiritual practice when it is performed
with the wisdom understanding the void nature of the three
circles: the giver, the gift, and the act of giving. This is generosity sublimated by the wisdom of non-duality; it is generosity
free of ego-grasping.

39

Who are the most poor
of all beings in this world?
Those so attached to their wealth
that they know no satisfaction.

We live in a world of infinite abundance, where wealth is a relative thing. A million dollars to one person is a fortune; to another it isn't enough to buy a decent house. A billionaire reduced to a mere millionaire may even commit suicide out of a feeling of desperate poverty, whereas an ordinary person who finds a few thousand dollars feels ecstatic.

The reality of wealth is that our attitude to our possessions is more important than the possessions themselves. Whether possessions make us richer or poorer depends on how we relate to them. The power of feeling wealthy is not in the wealth itself, but in our own mind. How we use what we have is more important than what we own.

The early Kadampa lamas had a saying, "If you have a miserly mind and one camel, you have the headaches of one camel; if you have a miserly mind and a hundred camels, you have the headaches of a hundred camels."

A simple person who has a positive attitude toward the few possessions he owns is rich; he lives in happiness and uses his wealth to benefit self and others. On the other hand, a wealthy person with obsessive attachment to his possessions is poor; his possessions bring happiness neither to himself nor to others. He worries about them, fears others due to suspecting that they are only interested in him for his wealth, and is uneasy even around his loved ones. He grows old suspecting that his relatives and friends resent him for his wealth and are anxiously awaiting his death in hopes of receiving an inheritance. He may even fear that his loved ones may murder him for it.

40

Who most infect the minds
of all the people they meet?
Those with harmful intent
but soft and cunning words.

Buddhism speaks of the body, speech and mind as being the three doors through which all our karmic energies pass. The mind is the most important of these three, for it determines the qualities of all actions of body and speech. That is to say, the actions we perform with body and speech are given a positive or negative quality by the mind; seemingly negative deeds done out of wisdom and compassion are in fact positive, whereas seemingly positive actions of body and speech are in fact negative when the mind performing them has a negative intent.

The Seventh Dalai Lama here likens soft and cunning words spoken with a harmful intent to a contagious disease. Just like someone with a contagious disease infects those with whom he comes into contact, negativity and confusion are most easily spread through sweet talk. That is to say, more harm is done in this world through clever, pleasant words spoken with a negative intent than is done through unpleasant words, for the negativity in them is packaged in an attractive wrapping. We can always see the negativity in unpleasant, abrupt words, and thus easily steer away from it; the danger from evil that is spoken with a cunning sweetness is more difficult to avoid.

41

Who seem most beautiful
to the worldly, samsaric people?
Those who act sweetly
and give their words like candy.

Here the Seventh Dalai Lama seems almost to laugh at the gull-
ible nature of most humans, for they generally look to style rather
than to substance. The people who act sweetly and speak with
candy-like words are usually taken at face value, and easily ma-
nipulate the masses. Their deeper motives are rarely examined.
They are like fishermen, who catch their prey by placing attractive bait on their hooks.

His words here are therefore a warning. We have to learn to
check the mind that is taken in by superficialities, and develop
the habit of a healthy skepticism. The Buddha recommended
that we be careful with all words, and always put everything we
hear to the test of reason, common sense and personal experience. When we fail to do so we leave ourselves vulnerable to the
machinations of duplicity. Then we have only ourselves to blame
when we are deceived and manipulated by others.

This verse may have an alternative interpretation. Ordinary
people are only able to respond to style, and have very little
sense of substance. This being the case, if we want to be liked
and appreciated by others we should be mindful of every word
that we say to them, and the manner in which we speak.

42

Who are most vain
of all beings in the world?
Those who use their wealth and friends
merely as external ornaments.

The essence of Buddhist practice is the transcendence of egoism and the false self. Our wealth should be used to benefit self and others in both mundane and spiritual ways, with the former being seen as a condition conducive to the latter. The integrity of the latter should never be sacrificed for an enhancement of the former, for this robs both of real significance and thus is self-defeating.

As for friends, they should be seen as beings with whom one shares positive karmic connections. One's friendships should be joint celebrations of the path to enlightenment, with a strong emphasis being placed on mutual benefit and growth.

When the basis of wealth and friendship is always kept on the firm ground of this enlightenment vision they will always be beneficial to both self and others. Conversely, when they are directed to the vain purposes of ego gratification they will bear little fruit in either worldly or spiritual spheres, bringing happiness in neither ordinary nor transcendental dimensions.

43

What is the target
of countless arrows of misery?
The temper of the mind unable
to bear even small ordeals.

The enlightenment path advocates practicing spiritual strength and humor in the face of the ordeals and challenges that life throws upon us. One is taught to see all difficulties, ordeals and challenges as teachers sent to help us learn more about ourselves, and to grow in inner stability and courage. Passing blame on to other people for whatever difficulties we encounter is seen as a weak and ineffective approach to accomplishing personal happiness, and results in frustration and unhappiness rather than personal growth and fulfillment.

The Indian master Shantideva said, "One person harms someone out of ignorance; someone else becomes angry out of ignorance. What makes the one blameless and the other an object of blame?" In other words, harming someone is caused by a lack of wisdom, and becoming angry at someone who harms is equally caused by a lack of wisdom. Why should we allow ourselves to embrace either mode, when both reflect ignorance?

Shantideva offers the following words of hope, "There is nothing whatsoever that is not made easy through familiarity. Practice patience with small difficulties, and thus gradually become patient with greater challenges."

When we allow the mind to flare up when it is confronted by ordeals and challenges, not only do we fail to meet the problem successfully. In addition we lay the foundations of a mind that is predisposed to fail in the future.

44

Ｗhat powerful demon
can topple even the strongest person?
Wavering, indecisive thought
unable to decide on the right course of
    action.

The mindset of indecisiveness is one of the twenty secondary
delusions. These twenty, together with the six root delusions,
comprise the twenty-six negative mind states in the list of fifty-
one "secondary minds" as set forth in the abhidharma teachings
of Buddhist psychology. In this picture of the mind we have six
primary minds, which are the five sensory consciousnesses plus
mental consciousness itself, and the fifty-one secondary responses. The twenty-six negative secondary mental states are
called "negative" because they produce unhappiness for self and
others.

Here the Seventh Dalai Lama likens the mind of indecisiveness to a demon that can topple even the strongest person; for
no matter how great our physical or mental strength may be,
when we are under the influence of indecisiveness we become as
though possessed by a ghost. All of our good qualities are tem-
porarily suspended, and they do not come back to us until the
ghost leaves or is exorcised.

In an earlier verse the Seventh Dalai Lama spoke of the importance of self-confidence. This is the opposite of the mind of
hesitation and indecisiveness. It is important to think before act-
ing, for this is the quality of wisdom. However, once a particular process has been thought through, it is equally important to
translate the conclusion into creative activity. Hesitation just
robs one of the dynamic power of accomplishment.

45

Who is the mule
braying his inferiority to others?
He who praises himself to others,
saying, "I have this and that good quality."

The early Kadampa lamas had a saying, "Speak only about the good qualities of others, and never about their faults. As for yourself, speak only about your faults and never about your good qualities." Also Geshey Potowa said, "Keep your own good qualities as secret as a treasure buried in your back yard."

The Seventh Dalai Lama uses the image of a mule, an animal that has a market value far lower than that of a horse. We may think ourselves to be a horse or even better, but as soon as we open our mouth with self-praise, everyone knows we are just a mule.

The commitment to humility in body, speech and mind was an instruction coming directly from the Buddha, who said, "Leave the announcement of one's own good qualities to those with delusions of grandeur." The eleventh-century lamas of the Kadampa school, to which all Dalai Lamas have a close affiliation, made this a prime principle. Their approach in this regard contrasted greatly with other schools of Buddhism in Tibet at the time, who saw self-elevation as one of the ways of promoting oneself as a teacher. The Kadampa way was soon emulated by the other schools, and became a strong national Tibetan characteristic.

The Dalai Lama link with the Kadampa school came because the First Dalai Lama lived in Nartang, one of the great Kadampa monasteries, from age seven until his early twenties, and received all his basic training there.

46

Who is the competitor
disliked by all the world?
He not respected by others
but who thinks himself superior.

Although we may compete with others in the spheres of career,
economics, romance, sports and so forth, there is no interper-
sonal competition in terms of inner character. Thinking ourselves superior to others just causes them to think of us as being a person of inferior character.

Humility free from pride is a sign of a great being. There is
no such thing as a proud buddha or saint. Pride and self-infla-
tion are qualities of the unenlightened. Not only do they obstruct one's spiritual progress, even on the worldly level they
are an impediment, invoking nothing but disrespect and ridicule in the minds of one's peers.

Tibetan Buddhism has numerous contemplative practices
known as *nyenpo*, or "remedies." One applies a specific remedial
contemplation to a specific delusion whenever it arises. Thinking oneself superior to others is one such delusion. Whenever
one feels lowly and inferior, one contemplates one's many blessings, and also contemplates the many living beings who find
themselves in inferior situations. Conversely, whenever one feels
superior to others, one contemplates all the great beings of the
world. In this way a balanced posture is established.

47

What is the great fault
that opens the door to all negative qualities?
Holding oneself more precious than others,
a characteristic of lowly beings.

In the Lojong (literally "mind-transforming") tradition of meditation common to all schools of Tibetan Buddhism one is taught to see the self-cherishing attitude as being the source of all unhappiness and suffering for both self and others. Eliminating the self-cherishing attitude is considered to be an indispensable step on the path to happiness and enlightenment.

The Indian master Shantideva pointed out, "Ordinary people cherish themselves more than others. Enlightened beings cherish others more than they cherish themselves. Look at the difference between the two! Which one do you think you should emulate?"

The First Dalai Lama advised that we cultivate the following thought: "The self-cherishing attitude has caused me to experience immeasurable suffering since beginningless time. Even now it continues to draw me into limitless suffering and confusion. And if I do not transcend it, it will continue to bring me misery without end. I should therefore make every possible effort to transcend it."

Lama Tsongkhapa said, "The essence of the Lojong practice is the mindfulness application known as 'exchanging self for others.' This does not refer to thinking that others are myself nor that the eyes and so forth of others are mine. Rather, it refers to taking the ordinary attitude that holds oneself as more precious than others, and exchanging it for the extraordinary attitude that holds others as being as precious as oneself."

48

What is like a smelly fart
that, although invisible, is obvious?
One's own faults, that are precisely
as obvious as the effort made to hide them.

Ordinary people try to hide their faults and show what they think of as their good qualities. However, the more we try to hide a fault the more pronounced it becomes. The only remedy is the transcendence of the fault. As long as it still holds sway over us it is definite that it will continue to manifest.

The first step in overcoming our faults is the arousal of the determination to face and acknowledge them when they appear. Ordinary beings don't do this, and instead try to hide them from both self and others.

Of course, not everything that causes us embarrassment is a fault to be transcended. Ordinary social conditioning sometimes makes us ashamed of things of which we should be proud, and proud of things of which we should be ashamed. For this reason it is important to examine one's situation closely and not just take one's spiritual tradition for granted. But when it looks like a fault, smells like a fault and feels like a fault, most probably it is a quality to leave behind.

The early Kadampa lamas likened the Dharma to a mirror, and said that the practitioner should look at his or her face in this mirror and then clean it up in accordance with what is seen.

49

Who, like the parrot, becomes trapped
by his own ability to speak?
He who talks recklessly
with no heed for the impact of his words.

The human ability to speak and communicate is considered to
be one of our greatest assets, for through it we can organize
ourselves into a very efficient society, and also pass on knowledge and information that is beneficial for both worldly success
and spiritual understanding. The transmission of Dharma, or
the spiritual knowledge conducive to enlightenment, is of two
types: the Dharma of transmitted realization; and the Dharma
of transmitted verbal instructions. The second of these is made
possible due to our ability to speak.

However, when we do not appreciate the power of our speech
it brings as many problems as benefits. Careless words said to
another can quickly induce anger, hatred and even violence. They
bring problems between family and friends, problems between
communities, and even problems between nations. Then, like the
parrot, we become trapped by our own ability to speak.

50

Who, like an old dog, becomes
more cantankerous when treated well?
He who fills with pride
when shown respect by others.

Lama Tsongkhapa wrote, "The more respect a wise person is shown, the more profound becomes his or her humility. With those of no spiritual qualification, however, the opposite is the case. For them, being shown respect just fills their minds with vanity and pride."

Also Geshey Potowa said, "For the spiritually immature, there is no greater pleasure than hearing the sound of their own name being praised. But for them this pleasure is like being spoon-fed poison; it just causes them to swell up with conceit." We shouldn't care whether we receive praise or criticism, other than perhaps to look at it for constructive feedback on something we have done.

In general we should take the advice that the Seventh Dalai Lama gave on another occasion, wherein he said, "Take the sounds of praise and criticism like you would take the sounds of your own voice echoed in a cave." In Tibet, practitioners would sometimes be instructed to go into a cave or canyon and alternately yell compliments and insults at themselves, listening to the echoed sounds and watching the mind's reactions to the praise and criticism.

These days, of course, we could make a tape recording of the barrage and just play it back to ourselves.

51

What is the one weed
that destroys the garden of happiness?
Mindlessness, that guards not
against negative karma of the three doors.

The one indispensable tool required for the path to enlightenment is mindfulness. It is this mental factor of acutely focussed
presence that makes possible the application of all the other di-
verse spiritual methods. Its opposite, i.e., mindlessness, or lack
of focussed awareness, is the one weakness that can allow all we
have accomplished to slip away.

The basis of spiritual practice is the observation of the energies flowing through the three doors, i.e., the body, speech and
mind, and the transformation of these from cyclic patterns to
enlightenment-oriented ones. Buddhism speaks of this process
as being comprised of the three higher trainings: discipline, meditation and wisdom. Self-discipline is the basis of the three, and
it is accomplished only by means of mindfulness of the transformations taking place through the three doors. This mindfulness is the force that makes the three trainings possible. When
mindfulness fails to maintain its strength, our practice soon falls
apart.

The Indian master Asanga likened the spiritual process to
growing a garden. When we have the proper amounts of water,
sunlight, fertilizer and so forth the garden grows beautifully.
Similarly for spiritual practice we need the appropriate applications in balance; then our spiritual garden grows well. Mindfulness is what empowers us to watch what is happening in our
lives and thereby maintain that balance. When we don't watch
our garden closely, the weeds can easily take over and destroy
all our efforts.

The Indian master Shantideva said, "A mad elephant cannot create the damage that can be created by one's own lack of mindfulness."

Also elsewhere the Seventh Dalai Lama said, "Mindfulness is the magic key that opens the door to all spiritual growth. Its opposite, mindlessness, is the heavy stone that drags us deeper into confusion and unhappiness."

52

What is it that makes one lose
everything one ever wanted?
Dissipating apathy, that fails
to persist in any task.

Apathy is the opposite of joyous energy or effort, the fourth of
the six Mahayana perfections. When we have joyous effort, all
works both spiritual and mundane are easily and quickly fulfilled. On the other hand when laziness and apathy set in, we are
not able to accomplish either worldly or spiritual goals.

Apathy is the quiet killer of human happiness. Due to it we
allow the precious minutes of our life to slip away, and our dreams
to slowly fade in front of our very eyes. Then before we know it
we are old and at death's gate, with only an empty, unfulfilled
life to look back on.

The Fifth Dalai Lama wrote, "Apathy is the greatest of
thieves. It steals the fruits of our success even before they have
been earned."

Apathy and laziness are eliminated by means of four main
forces. The first of these is joy. When we have a joyful appreciation for something, little room is left for apathy and laziness.
This joy can be aroused by meditating on the positive things in
the world. The second force is aspiration. Wanting something
in a pure and joyful way naturally inspires the creative energy
that dispels laziness. This aspiration can be aroused by meditating on the beneficial nature of the issue at hand. The third factor is mindfulness; when we watch the body, speech and mind
closely, the power of joyous energy is easily sustained. The fourth
factor is a suppleness of body and mind. When these two instruments are finely tuned and conditioned, laziness and apathy
automatically fade.

53

What force enters the life channel
and disrupts the stability of the mind?
The force called mental wandering,
that meanders in purposeless directions.

Tantric Buddhism speaks of the mind as being like a rider on a
horse, with the subtle energies of the body being like the horse.
When the horse is unstable, the rider will become destabilized.
Conversely, when the rider is unstable, the movements of the
horse will be disturbed.

The flow of the subtle energies is linked to the central channel and chakras of the body. The Seventh Dalai Lama uses the
image of an alien force obstructing the smooth flow of energy
in the central channel. This de-stabilizing force, he tells us, is
the wandering, unfocussed mind. Just as the qualities of the
subtle bodily energies affect the mind, likewise the flow of the
mind affects the flow of the energies. A vicious circle is created,
with the two working against one another rather than operat-
ing in harmony.

Meditation is a fundamental tool utilized in accomplishing
the path to enlightenment. The two principal obstacles to it are
mental wandering and torpor. For the novice in practice, the
former obstacle is the more dominant. Whenever we sit down
and place the mind on a subject of meditation, it soon begins to
drift off into different directions. Its lack of focus and concentration robs the meditation session of any real power.

A simple daily practice used by all schools of Buddhism for
increasing the stability and focus of the mind is to sit quietly
and watch the breath come and go, using a place of surveillance
such as the rising and falling abdomen. When thoughts arise

they are noted, and the mind then placed back on the breath. Doing this for ten or fifteen minutes once or twice a day greatly increases the mind's powers of concentration, as well as its emotional stability.

54

What cunning thief steals
cherished gems out of one's very hand?
Doubt, which is double-pointed
as regards spiritual practice.

Doubt has both a positive and a negative implication. It can serve as our friend and protector, but also can prevent us from entering into creative activity.

On the positive side, doubt in the sense of healthy skepticism breaks down our preconceptions and wrong understandings, and opens the door to new perspectives. Therefore Nagarjuna's great disciple Aryadeva said, "The mere thought of doubt causes the root of cyclic existence to weaken." Doubt eliminates the mind that takes things for granted, and forces us to look at them with fresh eyes.

On the negative side, doubt can rob us of spiritual vitality. Just as we cannot use a ladder effectively if we do not trust its strength, and a farmer will not plant seeds in spring if he does not trust the powers of nature to carry them through to a harvest, we cannot do anything effectively if we cannot develop a basic trust in the process.

The opposite of this negative sense of doubt is trust and confidence. This is to be developed carefully, and never allowed to degenerate into blind faith. As the Buddha put it about his own teachings, "Be like an analyst buying gold, and accept nothing on faith. Cut, burn and test these ideas in every way. Only accept what makes sense and proves beneficial."

The Seventh Dalai Lama uses the expression "doubt, which is double-pointed." This refers to a needle which is pointed at both ends, and has no hole to hold the thread. It cannot be used for sewing. Similarly, we cannot sew the cloth of spiritual practice with a mind that is pointed at both ends and has no hole for the thread of certainty.

55

Who is like the crazed war-elephant
that turns and destroys its allies?
He who holds negative thoughts
and harmful attitudes towards others.

In this verse the Seventh Dalai Lama borrows an image from Indian literature: that of the war elephant. Tibet did not have elephants, and therefore these magnificent animals were never used by Tibetan armies. In Europe elephants were first used for this purpose with great success by Hannibal in his surprise attack on Rome, a technique he learned from the Indians.

A problem with the war elephant, however, is that if it loses its composure and panics, it attacks whatever is nearest at hand, and this generally means the soldiers of its own army. The same is true of those who are dominated by anger and violence. They most frequently project their anger and violence upon their family and loved ones, who in reality are their main allies in life, and not their enemies.

In a larger sense, all living beings are our allies and therefore should always be treated only with love, compassion and understanding. Our life depends upon others both directly and indirectly. The food we eat is grown by others, transported by others, and sold to us by others. Without them doing this for us we would die. Similarly, our clothing and the material from which it is made comes from others, as does our house and everything else that we own. Medicines required in times of illness are made, transported and sold by others. Our education comes from others, and we inherit our language from people of past generations. Even the beings who try to harm us can bring great benefits, for the act of meeting hardships with patience and a good heart is an important spiritual exercise.

In fact, when correctly viewed, all beings can be seen as beneficial to us, and thus as allies. As a consequence, all should be treated only with love, compassion, tolerance and respect.

56

What deadly sword cuts off
all the branches of creative activity?
The sword of denial,
that does not face the reality of what is.

Philosophical denial is a major obstacle to happiness. It is the mindset that does not recognize the reality of a given situation, and thus fails to meet it with an appropriate response.

This type of denial mainly refers to our inability to appreciate the nature of causality and its dynamic presence in our every experience. Every experience that comes to us is a fruition of interconnected elements from the past. In turn, the way we deal with it creates forces that extend forever into the future.

As Buddha put it, "All things are interconnected. Those who truly see this achieve wisdom." When we ignore this basic principle, we are easily confused by the events that befall us, and weakened in our manner of dealing with them. Moreover, we do not give the individual moments of our life the attention or care that they deserve, for we fail to see the important role that they play in shaping our future.

57

What fishermen look for water
in dry, dead riverbeds?
Those who hope for spiritual progress
but cultivate neither wisdom nor positive
    energy.

These two factors—wisdom and positive energy—are known as "the two accumulations." All practices of enlightenment fall within one of these two categories, and all spiritual applications contribute in one of these two ways. When one eventually achieves enlightenment the former transforms into the Dharmakaya, the formless wisdom dimension of a buddha; the latter transforms into the Rupakaya, the emanated form dimension.

The "accumulation of wisdom" is cultivated by meditating on the non-duality of things, on how both self and phenomena lack any duality status, and are empty of any inherent existence. All other levels of wisdom have this singular vision as their ultimate aim.

The "accumulation of positive energy" is cultivated by means of all other enlightenment methods. The bodhisattva aspiration to highest enlightenment is the best such method. As the Indian master Shantideva put it, "When the bodhisattva aspiration based on love and compassion is fully integrated, one's every breath becomes a source of great accumulation of positive energy."

These two accumulations are often likened to the two wings of a bird, carrying us to enlightenment like a bird flying through the skies. Both are equally required, just as a bird needs two wings in balance.

58

 W hat is the mountain on which the faster
one climbs the faster one slips back?
Worldly possessions, that are spent
as quickly as they are laboriously acquired.

If the world ever enters into a golden age, it will probably look back on the present period of history with amusement; for these days the human mind seems to be obsessed exclusively with the accumulation of personal wealth. The result is that we are stripping our planet of its natural resources, destroying the environment, and undermining the very basis of life on earth. One of the reasons why Buddhists call the present era the *kaliyuga*, or "dark age," is that the aberration of greed is so pervasive that it is taken as normal.

The Buddha, like most other great spiritual teachers, advocated a life of material simplicity. We need good food, a decent dwelling, adequate clothing, a fulfilling job, and creative companionship. Beyond that, our needs are spiritual. Most people today close the door to the jewels of inner peace and happiness, and instead get caught up by the never-ending quest for material accumulation. In a world of infinite abundance, this never reaches an end.

Elsewhere the Seventh Dalai Lama wrote, "This body is a thing borrowed for a moment, and possessions are things stored for others. Now we dally with them, but soon they are lost; and, misused, they end only as sources of misery."

Also the Second Dalai Lama wrote, "Worldly works never reach an end, even if we struggle at them for an eon. Do not make them the center of your life. But spiritual practice is just the opposite, and every effort brings an according benefit that extends far into the future."

59

Who are empty-handed, even though
    having run
and searched throughout the three worlds?
The weakened living beings
tossed in samsara since beginningless time.

The previous verse addressed the problems of materialism; gathering "things" never achieves fulfillment, and in the end the person just dies and leaves all possessions behind. The only thing that travels on with us is the inner conditioning created on the mindstream by our thoughts, words and deeds during our lifetime. When materialistic hoarding is the priority in life, the karma will be mostly negative. Here the Seventh Dalai Lama points out how this fruitless endeavor continues lifetime upon lifetime until we break the chain.

The living beings are "weakened," for they have become conditioned by negative karma and delusion, and thus are predisposed to generate more of the same. The negative momentum perpetuates the cycles of repetition. They are "tossed in samsara since beginningless time," for karma and delusion have pushed them in circles since time immemorial.

The instruction to be gained from the verse, of course, is that we should make the effort to break the self-perpetuating cycles of karma and delusion in which we are enmeshed, and make the effort to achieve spiritual liberation.

This spiritual liberation is the subject of the verse that follows.

60

In what paradise of goodness and joy
is even the name "misery" unknown?
The state of supreme, peaceful liberation
beyond the compulsions of karma and
    delusion.

Early Mahayana Buddhist literature speaks of "pure lands" and
"buddhafields." These are synonymous terms, and refer to special paradises produced magically from the mindstreams of those
beings who have achieved enlightenment and become buddhas.
The number of these buddhafields is beyond count, although
historically only a half dozen of them received much literary
and spiritual attention. If one does not attain enlightenment in
this lifetime, achieving a rebirth in a buddhafield is the next best
thing. Each buddhafield is associated with particular meditational
and devotional practices, and these are utilized as a means of
creating the causes of a rebirth in that pure land. The two most
popular such paradises with the Tibetans are Sukhavati and
Tushita, the former being associated with Buddha Amitabha and
the latter with Buddha Maitreya.

Here, however, the Seventh Dalai Lama uses the concept of a
paradise as a metaphor for spiritual liberation. As he puts it, even
the word "misery" is transcended in the "state of supreme, peaceful liberation beyond the compulsions of karma and delusion."

The Thirteenth Dalai Lama said, "An ordinary being sees
this world as ordinary, and as a place filled with suffering and
confusion. An enlightened being sees it as a buddhafield." In
other words, every place in the universe is a paradise when the
mind of the experiencer is in the right place.

61

On what can one rely that has power
to protect from all forms of suffering?
The Three Supreme Jewels,
which no horror can affect.

The "Three Supreme Jewels," or *Triratna* in Sanskrit, refers to the Buddha, Dharma and Sangha. Every Buddhist has the commitment of reciting the words of taking refuge in these three spiritual forces three times a day and three times a night. Usually these are done at the beginning of one's morning and evening meditation sessions.

Historically the buddhas are the teachers, the Dharma is what they taught, and the Sangha are the advanced practitioners of those enlightenment teachings. A metaphor for this perspective on the Three Jewels is that the buddhas are doctors who prescribe the cure to the sickness of karma and delusion; the Dharma is the medicine that they prescribe; and the Sangha are the nurses who assist those who undertake the cure, i.e., who practice the enlightenment teachings.

On another level, the Buddha is our own omnipresent inner sacred quality, or buddha nature; the Dharma is the reality of being that is always at hand; and the Sangha is our aspiration or intent to draw on our inner buddha in order to attune to the nature of reality.

Tibetans often recite the following mantra as the basis of the "taking refuge" meditation: *Namo guru bhyeh; namo buddha ya; namo dharma ya; namo sangha ya.* In this mantra the guru is mentioned before Buddha, Dharma and Sangha, for he or she is the person who brings the Three Jewels into our life and unfolds them as realizations within our own mindstream. The guru is not regarded as a fourth jewel, but as an embodiment of all three jewels. On an inner level, the inner guru is one's ability to always bring the Three Jewels as a dynamic factor at play in every situation.

62

What is the crown jewel
That effortlessly fulfills all wishes?
A supreme master of the Great Way
Who guides one along the path to perfection.

In the Mahayana tradition the guru is seen as the embodiment of the Three Jewels of Refuge. The guru's mind is Buddha, speech is Dharma and body is Sangha. He or she is thus "the crown jewel." All spiritual and worldly aspirations are fulfilled when one relies on this guru. One accomplishes inner wisdom and joy, and in the outer world finds happiness, peace, prosperity, and harmony.

This guru is of four aspects. Firstly there is the ultimate nature of one's own being, which is the supreme teacher from whom one learns. Secondly there is the guru of one's ordinary experiences; i.e., one also grows in enlightenment by correctly reading the significance of one's own ordinary experiences. Thirdly there is the transmission guru; this refers to all the sublime instructions left by all the great beings of the past who have achieved enlightenment. Fourthly there is the living human guru, the accomplished spiritual masters from whom one receives guidance in the practice of the path.

By relying upon these four types of gurus—one's own ultimate nature, one's ordinary experiences, the sacred words of transmission, and the living masters—one easily and quickly attains enlightenment.

63

What is the currency of which one coin
can eradicate all types of poverty?
Spiritual conviction. No one can steal it,
and it dispels every mental confusion.

Buddhism speaks of three kinds of spiritual conviction.

The first of these is called "confident conviction," and refers to the trust and confidence that arises from an appreciation of the laws of cause and effect. A carpenter has to have confidence that the causal act of hitting a nail with a hammer will have the effect of driving the nail into the board. Similarly, we have to understand that everything we do is a causal factor that creates effects in our life; only then will we make the applications that lead to spiritual transformation.

The second type of spiritual conviction is called "aspirational." When we see something worth attaining and aspire to it, this driving force is a kind of trust that gives direction to our actions. In the spiritual sense, the aspiration is to accomplish the practices that produce enlightenment.

The third type of spiritual conviction is called "clear." This arises from meeting a great master and being profoundly inspired by him or her; or perhaps reading the words of an enlightened master and being profoundly moved by them. It is called "clear conviction," for the profundity of the impact of the experience arouses an intense clarity of mind that propels us in positive directions.

In spiritual life we need the confident conviction that we can accomplish the practices, the aspirational conviction that aspires to transformation and self-improvement, and the clear conviction that is inspired by the legacy of whatever path we are following. When these three are lacking, we sow with a needle with a point on both ends and no hole for the thread.

64

Who is the supreme friend
always helpful in times of need?
Mindfulness of the spiritual instructions
learned through study and contemplation.

Ordinary friends desert us when we fall on hard times or become an inconvenience in their lives. Others simply disappear into their own destinies. Even our spiritual teachers eventually die and leave us behind.

Our practice of the Dharma, however, that has been cultivated by means of study, contemplation and meditation, is the one sure anchor that keeps our ship stable when the seas become choppy. In fact, the more difficult the situation we encounter, the more helpful it is to us.

When the Buddha had become very old and was preparing to pass away, several of his disciples were overcome with grief. They asked him, "What will we do after you are gone?" He replied, "Whenever you rely upon my teachings, at that time I am there with you."

The Second Dalai Lama wrote, "When we know how to rely on the Dharma, we are able to be happy in every situation. Where could one find a more trustworthy and reliable friend?"

65

Where is the tranquil place
to rest the weary mind?
The bed of firm samadhi
undisturbed by mental wanderings.

The arousal of wisdom depends upon the force of successful meditation. This in turn depends upon the power of single-pointed concentration, or samadhi.

Maitreya said, "Samadhi arises by application of the eight antidotes that eliminate the five obstacles." In other words, to achieve samadhi we have to eliminate the five obstacles to successful meditation. These five are listed as follows: apathy; mindlessness; the twofold obstruction of mental torpor and mental agitation; not applying the antidotes to the obstructions when they arise; and applying the antidotes when they are unnecessary.

Eight antidotes are used to eliminate these five obstacles. Four of these eliminate apathy: appreciation of the powers of samadhi; strong aspiration to achieve samadhi; joyous effort; and relaxed, supple application. The antidote to mindlessness is the application of mindfulness. As for the third obstacle, which is constituted of the two factors of torpor and agitation, this is the main impediment to higher meditation. Its two factors are eliminated respectively by consciously sustained mental clarity and consciously sustained mental stability. Finally, the fourth and fifth obstacles are avoided by correct and restrained application of the antidotes.

The Seventh Dalai Lama calls the power of single-pointed meditation a "tranquil place to rest the weary mind." Here he is making a play on the Tibetan word *zhiney*, or *shamata* in Sanskrit. This is the form of mental training used to cultivate samadhi. The practitioner begins in retreat by performing eighteen short sessions a day, during which the mind is placed on one object, such as a visualized buddha-form, and not allowed to stray. The number of sessions is gradually reduced, and their length is increased. The stability of the mind increases, until eventually it is able to retain a single thought or visualized image for days at a time without either becoming sleepy or wandering away to other thoughts.

Samadhi by itself is a limited accomplishment, although it does unleash the clairvoyant powers of the mind. Ultimately, however, it is just a tool to be applied in the quest for wisdom.

66

What is the perfect eye that sees
all things in the world and beyond?
Clear wisdom, that distinguishes
the two levels of reality.

Buddhism speaks of two levels of reality. On the one hand there
is the ultimate reality of the emptiness nature of things, the
manner in which both self and phenomena lack any ultimate
status, inherent existence, or findable identity. Then on the other
hand there is the conventionally appearing, functional level of
self and phenomena.

A table, for example, is empty of any true existence. There
is nothing within or separate from the components of a table
that can be held up as "tableness." There is no tableness in the
wood, the varnish, or any other component; nor is there a
tableness separate from these parts. This is the ultimate reality
aspect of the table.

On the other hand, a table seems to exist, and seems to function in accordance with the laws of cause and effect. For example, we can sit down beside the table, put food on it, and enjoy
a good meal. This is the conventional reality aspect of the table.
The emptiness aspect is the ultimate reality of the table; the
functional appearance is its conventional reality.

Nagarjuna commented that searching for the meeting place
of these two aspects of reality is as dangerous as trying to pick
up a poisonous snake. Only when done correctly is the desired
result attained. The emptiness and conventional aspects must
be held in balance, or we fall into one of the two extremes, over-
shooting the emptiness side and falling into nihilism, or over-
shooting the conventional side and falling into reification.

An authentic understanding of these two levels of reality is what Nagarjuna meant by the *madhyamaka*, or "middle view." The attainment of that vision is a result of the three higher trainings of self-discipline, meditation and wisdom.

67

Who is the wise and skilled teacher
Guiding one away from places of negativity?
The force of mental attentiveness
awake to the realities of the moment.

Spiritual knowledge learned from books and from external teachers are useful sources of guidance in our life. However, they are limited in what they can do to help us. In the end, everything comes down to our own ability to integrate into our daily life what we have learned from them.

Mental attentiveness is an inner force that must be heightened and engaged in order for us to be effective in applying spiritual principles. Unless we are intensely aware of the flow of outer and inner factors at work in any given moment, and have the personal presence to respond appropriately, the greatest teacher and the highest teaching will be useless to us.

Therefore the Fifth Dalai Lama said, "You are your own best teacher. The best teaching is the one that is most appropriate to you in the moment. The indispensable condition by which these two best factors are accessed is the mental attentiveness of your own mind."

68

Who has such an intense discipline
that nothing can throw him from the way?
He in control of his own energies
who does not become stained with faults.

Spiritual practice is simple in that it is an application that is made moment by moment, like a complex painting that is executed stroke by stroke, or a long journey taken one step at a time. It is complex in that every moment brings its own adventures and challenges, each with its own unique character. The spiritual path is a matter of dealing with every circumstance in a such a way as produces happiness, wisdom, goodness and growth.

The Tibetan term that the Seventh Dalai Lama uses here for "intense discipline" is more often translated as "austerity," and is a carry-over from pre-Buddhist India. Many of India's pre-Buddhist traditions followed austere disciplines such as keeping one arm above one's head for, say, a year at a go; or only using one of the two legs for a similar period of time. One still sees yogis of this nature in India today. It is a useful tool in cultivating concentration, but the bodily limb itself suffers, often becoming completely shriveled because of never being used.

The Buddha discouraged such austerities when he taught the middle way. Rather than such external disciplines, he advocated the training of one's own mind. Therefore here the Seventh Dalai Lama replies to his question by saying that the supreme discipline is the monitoring of the karmic flows of one's own body, speech and mind, and the directing of them in positive ways.

Put in another Buddhist framework, it is the observation of one's body, feelings, thoughts and outer experiences, and the application of wisdom and compassion to whatever arises within these four spheres of experience.

69

Who is the best speaker
of all those strong beings?
He who has listened closely
to a vast range of enlightenment lore.

The eleventh-century Indian master Atisha once said, "This life is short, and the things that can be learned are innumerable. Be like the swan that, when it drinks milk, is able to separate the water from the cream, and to spit out the water and swallow the cream. In drinking knowledge, drink deeply of the cream, which is the enlightenment lore."

Ordinary worldly knowledge is useful, in that by acquiring it one learns something about some sphere of life. However, it does not affect the deeper levels of the mind, and only brings benefits on coarse or outer levels of being. Knowledge of the enlightenment lore, however, has the power to transform the mind at its very core. Murderers can become saints when they integrate it fully, as has been revealed many times in history.

This enlightenment lore is transmitted from generation to generation by means of both realization and words. The best form of listening is to hear the words of the enlightenment tradition from a fully realized master. One who speaks from that basis is a far better speaker than one who merely has oratory skills.

The Seventh Dalai Lama ties this verse to the previous one by using the expression, "of all those strong beings." Many people practice some form of spiritual discipline or others. The best teachers among them are those who trained under a qualified master.

70

Who are most respected
of all beings that exist?
The excellent ones with wisdom
not mistaken about reality.

With this and the previous two verses the Seventh Dalai Lama
builds a theme: discipline is good, but a discipline that directly
impacts the mind is better; ordinary learning is good, but spiritual learning is more quintessential; and, here, among those with
spiritual learning, those who have accomplished the realization
of wisdom are best.

Wisdom in this context does not refer to the mind of a wise
old man or woman in a general sense. Rather, it refers to the
heart of the wisdom taught by enlightened beings past, present
and future. This is the wisdom that directly and nonconceptually
sees how both the self and phenomena are by nature empty of
inherent existence, and are beyond the duality of having a separate and independent status. It is this insight that produces liberation from karmic patterns and both emotional and cognitive
distortions, and brings the joy of eternal freedom.

The Buddha said, "When one completely understands the
nature of being by means of the wisdom (of ultimate reality, or
emptiness), one transcends the three realms of confusion, and
achieves the state of utter liberation."

Also the Second Dalai Lama wrote, "This world we see is a
painting produced by the brush of discursive thought. Nothing
truly existent can be found within or upon it. All things in both
the world and beyond are but names and labels. Knowing this
one knows reality; seeing this, one sees most true." With these
few quintessential words he summarized all the Buddha's teachings on the cultivation of wisdom.

71

What is the loving behavior
inspiring to all people in the world?
Living an exemplary life
that accords with spiritual ways.

Two things happen every time we have an exchange with another living being: our behavior toward them leaves an impact
on their mind that is a conditioning factor in their evolution;
and their behavior leaves an impact on us that is a conditioning
factor in our evolution. In other words, we are constantly serving as a role model for others, and they for us.

The word that the Seventh Dalai Lama uses for "exemplary
life" is *yarab dampa*. *Yarab* means something like "elevated" or
"elevating," and *dampa* implies a sacred quality. The sense is that
some people use their precious human life to go from high to
higher, whereas some just squander the opportunity and pass
their lives in meaningless pursuits or even worse.

The opposite of *yarab* is *marab*. The former is a characteristic of truly spiritual people, and the latter, meaning "vulgar" or
"degenerating," is a characteristic of the spiritually uncivilized.
One can be highly educated, sophisticated, wealthy and successful in a worldly sense, and still be "spiritually uncivilized." When
that is the case all the outer glory is in vain, and one's life passes
meaninglessly.

In brief, the Seventh's message is that we should be mindful
that at every moment we are subtly changing history with our
actions, and shaping the destinies of those with whom we have
contact. The best way to express love and care for others is to
always maintain a quality of perfection in everything that we
do.

72

What is the sweetest conversation,
delighting absolutely everyone?
Gentle, appropriate words
built firmly on useful meaning.

The Indian master Nagarjuna used the image of four kinds of mangoes to illustrate the human situation. Some humans are green both inside and out; some are ripe inside but green outside; some are green inside but ripe outside; and some are ripe both inside and out. The best is to be in the fourth of these categories.

Harsh words based on attachment, aversion or ignorance is like the mango that is unripe both inside and out. Sweet conversation that is empty of meaning is like the mango that is ripe outside but unripe inside. Harsh words that are inspired by the wish to be beneficial are ripe inside but unripe outside. "Gentle, appropriate words built firmly on useful meaning," as the Seventh Dalai Lama puts it, are like the mango that is ripe both inside and out.

The Seventh uses the words "appropriate" and "useful." Truth is not as important as the appropriateness and beneficial nature of what is said. Words are only tools in communication. Their significance is not so much in what they say, as in the impact that they have on the mind of the listener and accordingly the results that they produce.

73

What is totally clean
and free of every taint?
The mind that has been purified
and is unmixed with the delusions.

The Buddhist hypothesis is that the mind can be utterly purified
of all faults and imperfections, and can achieve the exalted states
of final liberation and enlightenment. Once this has been accomplished the person graduates to the status of an *arya*, a transcended being.

The illustrious Indian master Nagarjuna likened the mind
to metal armor and likened the fire with which metal armor is
cleansed to the wisdom that brings the transcendence of imperfection. As he put it, "When metal armor has become stained, it
is placed in a fire and burned in order to clean it. The fire burns
off the stains, but does not harm the armor, which remains in-
tact. The same situation prevails with the mind. It becomes
stained by the delusions, such as attachment, aversion, and so
forth, and weighed down by the seeds of its own karmic instincts; but when it is burned in the fires of wisdom, only the
stains are destroyed. The mind's essential nature, which is pure
radiance, is not harmed."

Also the Buddha said, "One achieves liberation by realizing
the mind's primordially pure nature. When that wisdom is
aroused, the syndrome of grasping at duality in things is destroyed, all the afflictions and stains are released and mind arises
in perfect purity. This is the mind of an arya, and is the experience of nirvana itself."

74

What is the resolve
not undermined by others?
To guard oneself with awareness
against negative influences from others.

Every moment of our lives is a turning point. The direction we take with it opens up whole new karmic forces and patterns, reinforcing particular psychological tendencies and leaving others untried, and sending out energy fields that continue seemingly forever in such a way as to subtly shape our universe. Samsara occurs when we just unthinkingly repeat old response patterns; nirvana occurs when we bring peace into the present moment, and rather than respond blindly as a regurgitation of old habits we instead opt to rely upon higher awareness and critical intelligence. This latter is the wisdom that appreciates the relative manifestations of the moment, while simultaneously appreciating how they are empty of independent, true existence and are like the stuff of one's own dreams. As the Second Dalai Lama put it, "The things that appear to the mind are empty of a single atom of true existence; they manifest as dreams, and yet operate unfailingly by the laws of cause and effect." In other words, things seem to have a real, inherent presence, yet they are like illusions unfolding through the laws of interdependence and relativity.

The seemingly real world has no real existence, yet its presence is strongly felt by the mind which believes in its reality. Therefore those on basic levels of training closely observe the flow of conventional reality, the seeming realities of day-to-day experience. They keep the mind's awareness in the spheres of peace, joy and openness, while observing the flow of events from within the framework of the meditation on how the people and things that appear are empty of self-nature or findable existence, yet conventionally operate within the laws of interdependence and causality.

This is what the Seventh Dalai Lama means by the expression, "the resolve not undermined by others." One appreciates the conventional, operational presence of the events that appear to the mind, while looking in the face of emptiness; and while dwelling within the face of emptiness one shows respect for the conventional reality of causality and karma.

75

Who is the hero never beaten
by any external power?
The sage whose mind is never
lured by the things that glitter.

When the mind has not claimed an inner ground of peace and clarity, and has not achieved an awareness of the emptiness nature and potent presence of all things, it falls prey to the glitter that seems to emanate from both ultimate and conventional directions. In one's meditations on the emptiness nature of things one will be tempted to drift into the delights of meditative absorption; and in working with the conventional realities of day-to-day life one will be tempted to drift into attachments, aversions or complacency.

The former is less of a problem. The glittering aspects of emptiness meditation that can turn into distractions are usually rectified by the pressing needs of conventional life, such as eating and going to the bathroom. These bring one very quickly and naturally from the vision of emptiness to the conventional level of reality.

The problems of attraction to the glitter of conventional reality are more ubiquitous. Once one becomes addicted to one of them, there is no easy cure, other than the immense time required to eventually come to the understanding of the unfulfilling nature of the addiction. When the emptiness nature of phenomena is not appreciated, it is difficult to relate to anything on the basis of freedom from the mindsets of attraction, aversion or complacency.

For this reason the novice follows the threefold integrated methodology of self-discipline, meditation and wisdom trainings. This establishes a firm foundation. Eventually one achieves the stage of no-more-training, and sees all things as being void of the glitter of separate, true, findable existence; and yet sees that on the level of mere manifestation each phenomenon has a glitter unique unto itself.

76

What is the great army
able to defeat any enemy?
The power within oneself
of one's spiritual integrity and character.

As the Indian master Shantideva put it, beings in whom the mind of hostility prevail are to be found everywhere, and they can never all be eliminated. The simple solution is to tame the hostility within one's own mind. When this is done, the hostility of others rarely finds a target.

The Buddha said, "By taming one's own mind the whole world is tamed." Buddhists see any outer problem or conflict as being part of a bigger psychospiritual process. The actual appearing situation is only the tip of the iceberg of what is going on. The elimination of the outer problem is not as important as the tracing of its occurrence to one's own inner processes. Learning to confront the problem and understand it in relation to one's own evolution is crucial to growth and transcendence. Successful living is not so much a matter of efficient problem-solving as it is a matter of the psychology of problem appreciation. When the link is not made to one's own inner processes, any problem that is solved will just return in another form. On the other hand, when one solves a problem by means of seeing its psychospiritual significance, an entire dimension of problematic experiences is transcended.

The Tibetan term that the Seventh uses here for what I have translated as "integrity and character" is *yonten*. The word literally means something like "excellence" or "qualification," and refers to inner realizations of spiritual qualities like love, compassion, gentleness, wisdom and so forth. These qualities are like great mythological heroes that are able to face and overcome any hardship.

77

Who among those with strong self-confidence
need fear nothing that exists?
Those who have attained to truth
and are unstained by error.

The *Prajnaparamita* sutras speak of buddhahood as being a state
of utter fearlessness. To symbolize this, a buddha is often depicted iconographically as seated upon a throne upheld by eight
lions, the animal that more than any other living being embodies the experience of fearlessness.

   The Buddha once said, "He who fears when there is no need
to fear is a fool. He who does not fear when there is a cause of
fear is a fool. Both fall from the way." Self-confidence is generally a positive quality; but when it is not supported by the wisdom of enlightenment, it is often mere vain fancy. Therefore
the Tibetan yogi Milarepa once said, "Terrified of the eight
worldly concerns I fled to the mountains. There I meditated
unceasingly and gained wisdom. Now I no longer need fear."

   The Seventh Dalai Lama's expression "attained to truth" refers to the attainment of the wisdom of enlightenment, the consciousness that directly perceives the two levels of truth or reality: the ultimate reality, which is the void, emptiness nature of
all things; and the conventional reality of the infallible nature
of cause and effect. The being who has penetrated to the two
levels of reality transcends all distortion and delusion, and as a
consequence is never stained by error. Living each moment in
perfect harmony with reality, he or she has no need to fear anything whatsoever.

78

Who is like a rain cloud
enriching everything both near and far?
He who holds the mind in the thought
of bringing only benefit and joy to the world.

Here the Seventh Dalai Lama uses the words "enriching everything both near and far." Ordinary beings think to benefit those
who are near to them, i.e., their friends and family, but have no
such beneficial intent toward those who are far from them, i.e.,
those whom they regard as harmful or evil. In Mahayana Buddhism the emphasis is upon cultivating a universal attitude that
is above such discriminations.

The Seventh Dalai Lama wrote many tantric liturgies for
daily practice at the request of various disciples. Many of these
begin with the instruction, "First meditate on the four
immeasurables." Tibetans do this in conjunction with recitation
of the following words: "May all beings have happiness and its
causes. May all beings be freed from suffering and its causes.
May all abide in the joy which is free of suffering. May all abide
in that equanimity which is above attachment for the near and
aversion for the far." The rain cloud symbolizes this great equanimity, bringing benefit equally to those who are seemingly good
and those who are seemingly bad.

The Fifth Dalai Lama wrote, "We cannot determine how
other beings will behave. This depends on their wisdom or lack
of it. But we can determine that from our side we will treat all
of them with equal respect and care, regardless of their seeming worthiness or lack of it."

79

Who know that happiness
which is forever free of bondage?
Those who have released attachments
to the things that bind the mind.

A prerequisite of inner happiness is inner freedom. The attachment to objects, people and situations is the direct opposite of freedom. Insofar as a relationship is based on attachment, to that degree is our freedom constricted, and to that degree is the relationship unhealthy.

Mere attachment is in itself bad enough, but with it comes a host of other unhealthy emotions. These include anger at whatever is perceived as endangering the attachment, fear of loss, jealousy, and so forth. These crowd the space of the mind until there is no room left for inner peace or joy. In the end, the object of one's attachment turns one into a slave.

The modern Indian mystic Ramana Maharshi tells a wonderful story of a conversation between the ego and the stomach. The ego shouts at the stomach, "You terrible demon, you make me work and slave constantly in order to satisfy your insatiable needs." The stomach shouts back, "Actually, my needs are rather simple. But due to you and your attachments you keep me slaving from dawn to dusk without respite."

When the mind is dominated by attachment, the spirit rarely knows satisfaction, and even then only for very short intervals. On the other hand when the mind has transcended attachment it dwells in constant joy, no matter what objects, people or situations are at hand.

80

Who dwells in that sublime joy
that is unaffected by any adversity?
He who makes life's focus
the benefiting of all the world.

The former verse speaks of the fostering of inner peace and happiness in the context of the main object to be transcended, i.e., the mind of clinging and attachment. This verse speaks of it from the perspective of what is to be cultivated, namely, the mind that is focussed on universal good. When the mind is free from attachments it is able to experience peace and joy; similarly, when it dwells within the aspiration to be of benefit to the world, and thus remains free from egocentric concerns, it can maintain that inner peace and joy even when confronted with strong challenges and adversity.

This is, of course, only the conventional level of the picture. On a deeper level these two—freedom from attachment and from egocentric concerns—can only be fully achieved when one has aroused the wisdom that penetrates to the voidness nature of being. Ultimately the deepest source of freedom, peace and happiness is the wisdom of emptiness.

81

What is like the flying horse
well worth the trouble of seeking?
The status of a human being
endowed with strength and power.

The Tibetan myths of the flying horse are much like those of
the unicorn in Western culture. To see one is an exceedingly
rare and precious experience, an omen heralding the advent of
all things good and the fulfillment of all of our deepest aspirations. Similarly, reincarnation as a human being endowed with
full potential provides a most unique opportunity for achieving
the full perfection of final enlightenment.

In the above verse the Seventh Dalai Lama qualifies the status of a precious human being with the phrase "endowed with
strength and power." By this he means the eight freedoms and
ten endowments.

The Indian master Nagarjuna once said, "To achieve a human incarnation made rich with the eight freedoms and ten endowments is most rare. If there was a blind turtle living in the
ocean that came to the surface only once every hundred years,
and on that ocean there was a floating circular yoke, how rare it
would be for the turtle to rise with its head inside the yoke. A
human reincarnation is even more rare."

Lama Tsongkhapa wrote, "A human incarnation with the
eight freedoms and ten endowments is more precious than a
wish-fulfilling jewel. That magical jewel can make all worldly
wishes instantly come true; but a human incarnation is even
greater, for it can bring about the fulfillment of even the wish
for complete enlightenment."

The Seventh Dalai Lama speaks of the flying horse, and thus a human reincarnation, as being "well worth the trouble of seeking." The best is if we achieve enlightenment in this lifetime. Should we not succeed at this task, the next best is to achieve a human reincarnation and continue our practice in the life to follow. One ensures a human rebirth by having strong spiritual refuge, pure self-discipline, and profound aspiration.

82

What effort can be made
that will bring about some benefit?
Any effort, if it is made with creative presence
and graced with forethought.

Everyone wants to be a hero or heroine, and to enact a dramatic deed that will produce the beneficial for self and others. Deep inside, everyone wants to benefit the world. But just what is it that can be done? The Seventh Dalai Lama's suggestion is that we should attune ourselves to the needs of the moment, and on that basis respond with conscientiousness and forethought.

The Tibetan word here used for "creative presence" is *bak yo*. This is to be differentiated from the similar terms *drenpa*, usually translated as "mindfulness," and *shezhin*, usually translated as "alertness." *Bak yo* is the ninth of the eleven positive secondary minds (of the fifty-one secondary mental functions). It is defined as a wholesome mental agency that brings an attentiveness into the mind flow, a presence that has the function of sustaining the wholesome and avoiding the unwholesome. This mental agency is indispensable for developing stability and the power of higher meditative focus within the mind.

Thus the Seventh Dalai Lama is saying that any action is beneficial when it is based on the adherence of the mind flow to the fundamental principles of goodness, and when it is executed with the precision and care that accompany forethought.

83

What work, though done selflessly
best fulfills one's own aims?
Work based on the bodhimind,
and hence not distorted by self-cherishing.

The bodhimind, or in Sanskrit *bodhichitta*, is the very basis of
the Great Way taught by the Buddha. It arises from universal
love and compassion, is accompanied by the profound urge to
always be only of benefit to other living beings, and is sublimated by the aspiration to achieve full enlightenment as the best
means of fulfilling universal love and compassion. Lama
Tsongkhapa called it "the one path all buddhas past, present
and future have walked, do walk and will walk," for it is the basis
of mental/spiritual experience that gives rise to enlightenment.
Anyone in any age or place who achieves enlightenment does so
as a natural unfoldment of the bodhimind experience.

In Buddhist scriptures the methods advocated for arousing
the bodhimind repeatedly use the words "for the benefit of all
living beings." For example, texts on Lojong practice recom-
mend that we begin every activity with the conscious prayer
that the deed may be of benefit to all living beings. We should
maintain this altruistic thought throughout the activity, and at
the conclusion dedicate any positive energy that was generated
to the attainment of enlightenment for the benefit of all. Similarly, a liturgy often used to arouse the bodhimind at the beginning of a tantric meditation session states, "In order to quickly,
quickly attain highest enlightenment as a means of being of
greatest benefit to all living beings, I now engage in this tantric
method."

The Seventh Dalai Lama here is pointing out that this manner of always meditating on being of benefit to others in fact brings the greatest benefit to oneself. The more one generates love and compassion, the happier and more fulfilled one becomes; the more one replaces self-cherishing with universal concern, the more one brings benefit to oneself.

84

Who is the best role model
with advice that should always be heeded?
He who has established inner control
and speaks with words both gentle and true.

Inner control here refers to two things. Firstly, it implies that the attitude that holds self above others has been reduced and has been replaced with universal love and compassion. Secondly, it implies that the wisdom that perceives the emptiness nature of being has been aroused, and thus the mind of grasping at the false self has been calmed. Consequently the "inner control" that has been established is not a forced act of stoic will power, but rather is a relaxation of the negative mind and a leaning into what is universally true, good and beneficial. The person who has accomplished this timeless deed is a true and reliable role model.

The Seventh Dalai Lama adds, "and speaks with words both gentle and true," for we cannot really know who does and does not have inner spiritual realization. All we can know is the outer expression exhibited by the person. His or her behavior should be in accord with the exemplary lifestyles set by the great masters of the past. We have no way, other than by examining their words, to know how deep this outer expression runs.

Similarly we ourselves should emulate the tradition of always keeping our words gentle and true.

85

What is the precious and rare medicine
that kills the appetite but revives the spirit?
True and beneficial words
spoken by others in challenge of one's faults.

A twelfth-century Kadampa master once said, "Whenever you
find a fault in yourself, rejoice like someone who has discovered
a precious treasure. Having found and faced it, you now have
some hope to overcome it. Otherwise, hiding from or burying it
will never cause it to go away."

Ordinary people react to personal criticism by becoming de-
fensive or even angry. In the Lojong tradition one always cultivates the opposite of the ordinary. In this case it means reacting
to criticism with openness and appreciation.

The Second Panchen Lama, who was one of the gurus of
the Seventh Dalai Lama, suggested that we regard those who
criticize us as being emanations of our spiritual teachers. He
went on to explain that by doing so, one not only avoids the
negative karma created by succumbing to anger and resentment,
but in addition opens the door to learning something about oneself. The criticism may contain some truth from which one can
benefit.

The Indian master Shantideva pointed out that receiving
criticism with composure is an excellent practice for purifying
the mind. Not only does it reduce pride and egoism, but in addition one's karmic predisposition to be the brunt of someone's
attack is brought to the fore. By dwelling in calm observation
of the process and meditating on the emptiness nature of the
three circles—the one criticizing, the one being criticized, and
the act of criticism—the karmic seed is uprooted and destroyed.

86

What is like a powerful ambrosia
of which one can never drink enough?
The sublime oral instructions
that reveal the inner meaning of Dharma.

As mentioned in the Introduction, the great Indian master
Atisha, who brought the Lojong tradition of Buddhism from
Indonesia to Tibet, placed a strong emphasis upon the study
and practice of quintessential oral transmission teachings as
opposed to the *zhung chen*, or great Buddhist classics. Oral instruction lineages generally tend to combine various teachings
of the Buddha and update them in accordance with their
formulator's direct experience. Thus they are more immediately
transformative than are the more formal transmissions.

The Seventh Dalai Lama calls these orally transmitted lineages "a powerful ambrosia," for just as the ambrosia of the gods
heals the full range of illnesses and immediately rejuvenates the
body of the person who has the good fortune to acquire it, in
the same way the oral transmission lineages easily heal a practitioner of the full range of mental/spiritual distortions as well
as the instincts of negative karma, and also bring the complete
rejuvenation of enlightenment.

Every school of Tibetan Buddhism has numerous oral transmission lineages. Some of these come from India and other countries from which Tibet acquired its Buddhist legacy; others were
formulated by great Tibetan lamas who achieved enlightenment.
Most Tibetans today train in one or more of these, while simultaneously complementing their practice of the oral transmission with a study of the great classics.

87

What is the supreme jewel
to be most carefully guarded?
The essence of what has been heard,
that, when relied upon, brings transformation.

The theme of this verse is a continuation of the former one,
wherein the Seventh Dalai Lama pointed out the importance of
receiving many experiential spiritual instructions and discourses.
Here he points out that what we have to do, after hearing the
teachings, is put them into practice. Hearing the instructions on
the enlightenment methods is a powerful medicine; but just as a
patient must take the remedy prescribed by the doctor in order
to experience the cure, likewise we must integrate the essence
of what spiritual instructions we have learned, and must put
them into actual practice, if they are to have the desired effect.

The Fifth Dalai Lama once wrote, "It is better to learn one
spiritual method and practice it well than it is to listen to many
instructions and not put them into practice." Also the great master Sakya Pandita said, "In the beginning one should listen to
many instructions. In the middle one should deeply contemplate
their meaning. In the end one should thoroughly integrate them
by means of meditation."

The Seventh Dalai Lama uses the idea of guarding our practice like we would guard a precious jewel. In Buddhism the sole
responsibility for our spiritual progress lies in our own hands,
just as the owner of a jewel is responsible for its safety. If we are
careless, the jewel can easily be lost. Similarly, if we do not take
responsibility for keeping our practice together then it will easily fall into the sphere of empty words.

88

Who holds in his hands
the seeds of every joy?
He with vast stores of goodness,
the source of everything sublime.

The word used here for "stores of goodness" is *sonam*, or in Sanskrit *punya*. Tibetan Buddhism divides its practices into method and wisdom; the method applications generate *sonam*, often translated as merit, and the wisdom applications generate insight. Sonam is the basis of the positive karmic energy that gives rise to every conducive circumstance, and thus to the happiness or joy experienced by the mind; wisdom gives rise to the freedom within the mind by which that joy can be directed toward higher transcendence. Sonam has much the same meaning as "positive karma," although something of a different referent.

As said in the commentary to verse fifty-seven, these two aspects of spiritual application are sometimes referred to as "the two accumulations." The Mahayana Buddhist accumulates stores of goodness, or merit, and also accumulates wisdom, or insight. The former eventually emerges as the form body of enlightenment, and the latter as the wisdom body.

Put in another way, the first five of the six bodhisattva "perfections" are method, and the sixth is wisdom. Thus the first five contribute to merit, and the sixth to insight. This is the manner in which the eleventh-century Indian master Atisha spoke of the matter.

An earlier Indian master, Chandrakirti, stated that the first three perfections (i.e., generosity, discipline and patience) are linked to method (and thus merit), and the sixth directly to wisdom (and thus insight). This leaves the fourth and fifth perfections (i.e., joyous energy and meditative stabilization), which he stated become either method or wisdom depending on their focus. When they are used in conjunction with the first three perfections they become merit factors, and when used in conjunction with the sixth perfection they become wisdom factors.

89

What supreme possession
brings its owner everything beneficial?
The practice of Dharma, for it protects
from every negativity.

One of the definitions of Dharma, or spiritual application, is
"that which protects the mind from suffering." In other words, a
method is only truly spiritual if its application extracts the
mindstream of the practitioner from negative karma and afflicted
emotions, the two causes of suffering. So-called spiritual methods that fail in this regard are but diversions. Any method that
effects this extraction is Dharma.

The word *dharma* is often translated as "religion." However,
the above definition of the term suggests a broader meaning.
Because of this rather large and encompassing attitude,
Mahayana Buddhism has rarely developed a policy of exclusiv-
ity to truth as has so often been exhibited by the three Semitic
religions—Judaism, Christianity and Islam. Instead, it tends to
see different spiritual traditions as offering different means for
extracting living beings from the web of suffering that pervades
unenlightened existence.

Practice of the Dharma protects one from negativity on the
conventional level by mitigating the activity of bad karma and
delusion; and on the ultimate level by inducing the wisdom which
perceives the non-dual nature of being, and thus the insight that
uproots grasping at the self as having a separate and independent status.

90

What is an auspicious omen
in country and city dweller alike?
Love, that seeks harmony amongst people,
and that wishes only happiness for others.

The term that the Seventh Dalai Lama uses here for harmony is
puntsun yitu ongwa, which literally means "seeing one another
with affection." The *yitu ongwa* segment of the expression literally means "delighting the mind," and is likened to the way a
mother reacts to seeing her only child. The mere sight of the
child brings pleasure and joy to the mind of the mother.

The quality of mind that always delights in the company of
others, and that only wishes them well, is an "auspicious omen"
in a person. Just as an auspicious omen seen in cloud formations,
dreams or the like is a prophecy of good things to come, the
quality of mind that always looks on others with affection and
sympathy is an indication that the possessor of that mind is des-
tined for happiness. When one has established the mind that
always looks on others with love, one's experience of the world
becomes more loving, peaceful and fulfilling.

The Buddha said, "The presence of love in the mind immediately pacifies whatever negative energy is present in one's environment. The force of the delusions is weakened, and the iron
grip of negative karma is loosened."

91

What is to be most closely guarded
when one is in a crowd?
The actions of body and speech,
both of which are determined by the mind.

This and the verse that follows are reiterations of the eleventh-century saying by the Kadampa lamas, "When in public watch all movements of body and speech. When alone, watch all movements of the mind."

All of our karma, both positive and negative, flows through these three doors. We experience the world by taking in energy through them, and impact the world by sending out energy through them. Whatever control of our destiny that we claim can only be established by taking control of the movements that occur within these three.

The Kadampa lamas suggested that when we are alone we use the peace and quiet to sit in meditation and observe the deeper levels of our own mind. Then when we are in the company of others we should change our focus from the transformations of mind to the activities of body and speech, for these reflect the progress or lack of it that is being made through the work with the mind.

92

What is the thing to be guarded
that is the basis of help or harm?
The state of one's own mind,
the basis of both good and evil.

Although observing the activities of body and speech can
help us to understand ourselves and improve the quality of our
life, these activities emanate from the mind itself, and therefore
understanding the mind is of paramount importance to someone seeking lasting happiness.

The Seventh Dalai Lama calls the mind "the basis of both
good and evil," because whether we use our life to benefit or to
harm self and others depends upon the state of our mind. For
that reason the Buddha spoke of the mind as being an unspecified phenomenon, in the sense that it is not specifically either
positive or negative. When a person allows negative factors such
as anger, jealousy, attachment and so forth to dominate, the mind
becomes negative. The person then is driven by these negative
forces and enters into negative activity of body and speech, bringing harm and suffering to self and others. That unspecified mind
thus becomes evil. Conversely, when one guards against these
negative mental agencies and instead cultivates their opposites,
such as love, compassion, tolerance, forgiveness and so forth,
one becomes driven by these positive forces, and one's mind can
be spoken of as being a positive phenomenon.

We all carry on our mindstreams the seeds of both positive
and negative karma, and thus have the potential to be both good
and evil. That is the case until we achieve the higher wisdom by
which the power of inner karmic instinct is transcended and

spiritual liberation is achieved. The Seventh Dalai Lama advises us to keep constant watch of the flow of our mind until that wisdom has been attained and also as a means of generating that wisdom.

93

Who are honored as elders
by every being that lives?
Those with the light of the wisdom able
to distinguish the essence of being.

The Tibetan phrase used here for "essence of being" is *jawai ney*, which literally means "the crux of activity." This crux is like a coin with two sides to it.

On the one hand there is its unfindability, the void nature of its three circles. There is no findable doer, no findable action which is done, and no findable object of that activity. All three of these circles have no true, separate, inherent or findable reality, no self-nature. They exist merely conventionally as mental labels and imputations. Alternatively, in the language of the Mind Only school, they are merely of the substance of one's own mind. Understanding all things in this way instills a person with what the Indian master Chandrakirti called "the great tolerance." When one sees all things as mere labels, one develops a mindset characterized by great gentleness, smoothness and patience.

On the other hand there is the conventional appearance of the phenomenon or event, which is its functional level of existence. There may be nothing within or about it that has any true reality status, but nonetheless in the minds of those who grasp at true existence it behaves as though it is real. On the conventional level, the laws of cause and effect hold true.

Those who appreciate these two sides to everything that appears are illuminated by the light of wisdom, and deserve to be respected as true elders by all living beings.

Old people who lack this wisdom should be shown respect merely for having survived life's rigors. However, they are not truly elders, but as the Seventh Dalai Lama puts it in another of his writings, are "children who are deceived by the mere appearance of things."

94

Who amongst those who have achieved
    human rebirth
have found the most meaningful livelihood?
Those who dedicate their days and nights
to goodness and happiness for all.

The Buddha described the path to enlightenment in many ways. One of these was the noble eightfold path as taught by the aryas: right vision, right understanding, right speech, right action, right livelihood, right aspiration, right mindfulness, and right samadhi.

He stressed the fifth of these, which is right livelihood, as being an especially delicate concern for the layperson. Monks and nuns in traditional India lived by collecting alms once a day, i.e., begging, and thus for them right livelihood was a simple matter. Other vows of the ordained sangha, such as not touching or handling money, further ensured that they would maintain a simple lifestyle.

For the layperson, however, the external situation is much more complicated. The demands of paying rent, supporting children and elders, and maintaining an entire material world creates a situation in which it is very easy indeed for negative attitudes, energy and activities to creep in. As Lama Tsongkhapa put it, "Everyone loves family and friends. Unfortunately, many people create much negative karma in order to benefit their loved ones, and in order to harm those whom they consider to be a threat to them."

The Seventh Dalai Lama suggests a simple means whereby the layperson can always maintain right livelihood: dedicate every activity both day and night to the goodness and happiness of the world. Bringing this basic focus into every action automatically transforms it into something positive and wholesome.

95

Who are most wise
amongst the learned beings of the world?
Those who use their hands
to take up and put down what is appropriate.

The Tibetan expression for "take up and put down" is *lang dor*, an earthy metaphor for the process of moment-by-moment living. Every moment of our lives we are taking something up and putting something else down.

Lang dor could alternatively be translated as "take and leave." Every moment we have to decide how to deal with the situation with which we are confronted. The response that we choose is what we "take," and the paths we do not take are what we "leave."

The responses of ordinary beings to the situations with which they are confronted are usually unconscious and instinctual. As Buddhists would put it, they are "based on karmic predispositions." In other words, they are cyclic in nature, and thus the mere re-living of old patterns.

Those following a spiritual path learn to by-pass the unconscious and karmically instinctual manner of dealing with things, and instead interject a spiritual awareness or discernment into the process. In other words, they learn to bring wisdom into their lives.

Of all learned peoples, the wise are those who learn to bring the knowledge they have acquired into the task of transforming their own lives. They become enabled to see the choices that lead to the road of higher being and transformation, and to leave behind those patterns that obstruct happiness and growth.

96

What is that harm
not to be inflicted upon others?
The very harm one would not
like to have inflicted upon oneself.

The Seventh Dalai Lama's words here are somewhat reminiscent of the instruction by Jesus—"Do unto others as you would have them do unto you." The Seventh, however, states the idea in the form of a double negative: "Do not do unto others what you would not have them do unto you." Jesus' phrasing would be what Buddhists call universal love, i.e., the aspiration that others have happiness. The Seventh Dalai Lama's phrasing would be what Buddhists call compassion, i.e., the aspiration that others be free from suffering.

The essence of the Great Way taught by the Buddha is the doctrine of universal compassion. As the Third Dalai Lama put it, "All the great masters of the past have, after their enlightenment, taught the path to inner peace and joy not in order to benefit themselves but in order to benefit living beings. They elucidated the enlightenment methods solely out of compassion. If we ourselves practice what they taught, we should honor this commitment to compassion and always practice it ourselves. At the very least, we should never bring unnecessary harm to living beings."

97

What is the supreme goodness
always beneficial to others?
Pacifying and completely subduing
one's own difficult-to-tame mind.

There are many little things that we can do to benefit the world, such as volunteer work in our community, contributing to our favorite charities, becoming involved in noble political causes, and so forth. However, as good as any of these may be, by themselves they are of limited value. As long as our own mind is controlled by the I-grasping ignorance and does not understand the infinity of our own being, we will continue to be plagued by attachments, anger, jealousy, pride and the host of other delusions. As a result we will continue to enter into actions based on these distorting forces and will bring harm to self and others.

The supreme act of volunteer work is to volunteer to achieve the enlightenment mind; the supreme charity is to give the world one's own transcendence; and the supreme political cause is one's own liberation from karma and delusion. When this is the focus, all one's other good works become meaningful.

98

What is the supreme treasure
that can never be exhausted?
Giving without expectations
to the sublime or to the needy.

With this verse the Seventh Dalai Lama begins his treatment
of the six bodhisattva perfections, or six transcendences: generosity, self-discipline, patience, joyous energy, meditative stabilization, and wisdom. As the Indian master Nagarjuna put it, "The
path of all the buddhas—those past, present and yet to come—
is exclusively that of the (six) perfections."

The Sanskrit name for "perfection" is *paramita*, or "gone beyond," because the six transport the practitioner beyond ordinary samsaric experience. Moreover, all six are practiced together, and thus are sublimated by the sixth, which is wisdom;
in this sense they are "beyond the world."

For this reason the "six transcendences" would perhaps be a
more accurate translation than "six perfections." However, a hundred years of Western Buddhism have made the latter rather
firmly entrenched in the Western mind.

The Seventh Dalai Lama terms the practice of generosity a
"supreme treasure," for through it one benefits both oneself and
others. An act of generosity is a source of joy not only to the
recipient but also to the giver. Whereas miserliness reinforces
personal insecurity, and also prevents a person from enjoying
what he or she possesses, generosity encourages the appreciation of what one has and facilitates its enjoyment. In fact, the
very enjoyment of material things comes from generosity. As
the great Lama Tsongkhapa put it, "The perfection of generosity is a magic gem to fulfill the hopes of the world, the best of

tools with which to cut the knot of avarice that constricts the heart, the bodhisattva deed giving birth to the unfailing powers of the spirit, the foundation of beneficial reputation."

The perfection of generosity based on universal love and compassion is practiced in three ways. This was stated by the Third Dalai Lama as follows, "The practice of the perfection of generosity means giving material things, good counsel and/or protection from danger, and doing so on the basis of a pure and free heart." The emphasis is on the purity and freedom of the heart.

99

What magical ritual destroys
the most vicious of demons?
Self-discipline, which tethers itself
far from faults of body, speech and mind.

The second of the six paramitas is that of discipline. This perfection is defined as a mental agency that is determined to avoid
what is harmful to self and others, and to accomplish what is
beneficial. The three types of discipline mentioned in Buddhist
literature are the discipline of avoiding harmful activities, the
discipline of accomplishing wholesome activity, and the discipline of working to benefit others.

The Buddha said, "Just like the earth is the foundation on
which living beings cultivate all their food, discipline is the
ground that preserves and increases all good qualities, including meditation and wisdom." In other words, discipline is the
basis of all spiritual growth.

Lama Tsongkhapa comments, "Ethical discipline is water to
wash away the stains of negativity, moonlight to cool the heat
of delusion, radiance towering like a mountain amidst living
beings, and the force that peacefully unites mankind. I, a yogi,
cultivated it myself. You who seek liberation should do likewise."

100

Who armor is never pierced
by any type of weapon?
Patience in the face of challenges
arising from insults and attacks.

The third of the six perfections of the bodhisattva path is that
of patience. Here one trains oneself to be gentle and relaxed in
meeting the three types of ordeals that are encountered in life:
harm from other living beings; the aches, pains and challenges
that life occasionally throws at us; and the difficulties encountered while cultivating a spiritual practice.

Lama Tsongkhapa said, "Patience is the best ornament of
real heroes, a supreme austerity to overcome afflicted emotions,
an eagle that destroys the snake of anger, and armor to protect
one against arrows of harm. I, a yogi, cultivated it myself. You
who seek liberation should do likewise."

The Indian master Shantideva stated that the supreme
method for cultivating the inner quality of natural patience is
meditation on the void nature of the three circles of the experience: oneself as the practitioner of patience; the object that is
arousing one's ire; and the practice itself. All three of these have
no real existence and are mere illusions drawn by the brush of
conceptual thought. They are mere mental labels and imputations, and are utterly empty of inherent existence.

The present Dalai Lama once suggested to me that a useful
conventional method of developing patience is to cultivate the
habit of looking at the uselessness of the hostile mind whenever it arises. Remind yourself that the object of irritation is a
problem to be solved, like a mathematical equation. Just as clear
and sustained thought is more effective than anger in solving a

mathematical equation, so the problems that confront us in life are more effectively solved with a gentle and relaxed mind than they are by a mind that reacts with the blindness of anger and hostility.

101

Who has the magical horse
able to go wherever reined?
He with joyous energy
that tirelessly completes every undertaking.

The fourth perfection is that of joyous energy or effort. It is defined as a mental agency that delights in wholesome endeavors.

There are three aspects of this paramita: armor-like joyous energy, which has the confidence to engage in all creative activities and can face any obstacle without wavering; joyous energy in wholesome endeavors, which never tires of creative effort; and joyous energy in working to benefit others.

Joyous application is here likened to armor. Just as a suit of armor protects a soldier against the arrows and swords of hostile warriors, this paramita provides one with strong protection against all challenges and obstacles. When one's effort is naturally joyous, the most powerful hindrance seems small. One becomes like a warrior in battle, who grows in strength and determination from any wounds that he receives.

In general we usually fail at the tasks we undertake simply because we submit to failure, and not because our efforts have not succeeded. This paramita instills in us the courage to face all tasks with joy and enthusiasm. Lama Tsongkhapa said, "When one dons the armor of joyous effort, qualities of learning and insight grow like the waxing moon. All activities become meaningful, and all works undertaken reach completion. I, a yogi, cultivated it myself. You who seek liberation should do likewise."

102

What is the sparkling mirror
reflecting even invisible images?
The firm yoga of meditative quiescence
not disturbed by agitation or torpor.

The fifth paramita is that of meditative absorption, or *dhyana* in Sanskrit. It is this term that became translated as *ch'an* in Chinese and *zen* in Japanese, giving rise to the Buddhist schools of those names.

Meditative absorption is described as a stable and focussed state of mind that has evolved from mindfulness and awareness. It is an indispensable prerequisite for the cultivation of deeper insight into emptiness and the void nature of being.

The three types of meditative absorption are the absorption that unites investigation and analysis; the absorption with analysis but no investigation; and the absorption that is without both.

Lama Tsongkhapa praised this extraordinary mental power as follows, "Concentration is the king that rules the mind. When stabilized, it sits like a mountain; when directed, it can enter every creative sphere. It leads to every physical and mental joy. I, a yogi, cultivated it myself. You who seek liberation should do likewise."

The Indian master Shantideva emphasized the importance of meditative absorption, and said, "A person with an unfocused mind is constantly between the fangs of the afflicted emotions. Therefore keep the mind focussed." When our meditative power is weak, the negative forces of anger, attachment and so forth find us to be an easy target. Meditation cannot eliminate these forces, but it can mitigate them. The process of elimination is accomplished by the sixth perfection, that of wisdom.

103

Who flies unobstructedly
throughout the boundless skies?
He with a mind focussed on the void,
and who thus is forever free of hindrances.

Finally, the sixth perfection is that of wisdom. This refers to the awareness of the non-duality of things, the emptiness nature.

This wisdom is of three types: worldly wisdom, transcendental wisdom and the great transcendental wisdom. The first refers to the wisdom that has not yet achieved the non-conceptual experience of the emptiness reality; the second refers to the wisdom of someone who has achieved that direct experience; and the third refers to the wisdom that is free from all obscurations, and is realized only at the time of full enlightenment.

This wisdom directly uproots all distorted states of perception, all the delusions and afflicted emotions, the seeds of all negative karma, and all instincts of distortion. It induces the direct experience of the nirvana of buddhahood, and the according liberation from samsara.

Lama Tsongkhapa says, "Wisdom is the eye which sees things as they are, the application that severs conditioned existence at its root, the treasure of excellence praised in all scriptures, and the supreme lamp to dispel ignorance. I, a yogi, cultivated it myself. You who seek liberation should do likewise."

Lama Tsongkhapa points out that this wisdom is best induced by means of combining meditative absorption and awareness of the void. As he puts it, "The power to cut the root of conditioned existence does not lie in single-pointed concentration alone; and awareness of emptiness divorced from meditative concentration will not eliminate the force of the delusions and distortions, though it may try. Wisdom searching for ultimate reality should ride the horse of unwavering samadhi, and with the sharp weapon of centralized thinking should totally destroy grasping at 'is' and 'is not.'"

104

What is the most amazing drama
to be seen even in dreams?
The scenes that appear to the senses,
and that should be understood as illusions.

During formal meditation sittings one absorbs the mind in samadhi upon the emptiness nature of all that exists, the manner in which all things lack an inherent, separate nature. After meditation, when one arises from one's meditation cushion and enters the ordinary world, the awareness of non-duality that was generated during the meditation session has the after-effect of causing the world that appears to the senses to assume an illusory, dream-like quality. One reinforces this subtle effect by maintaining a strong mindfulness of how all things appear as though having self-nature, yet in fact lack any duality status whatsoever, like illusions, hallucinations, and the objects of a dream.

Lama Tsongkhapa said, "During sessions meditate single-pointedly upon space-like emptiness. Between sessions, see all things as a magician's creations. Through familiarity with these two practices, wisdom and method are perfectly united, and one arrives at the end of the bodhisattva path. Understand this point clearly, and always keep method and wisdom in balance. Discover this road of the fortunate. I, a yogi, cultivated that myself. You who seek liberation should do likewise."

The Second Dalai Lama suggested that we offer the following prayer, "During meditation may I attain the naked insight that perceives the emptiness nature of all that exists, how all the appearing and transforming phenomena have no real existence whatsoever, and are mere imputations of the conceptual mind. Between sessions, may I carry this insight into my daily activities, and observe all the things that appear to the six senses without grasping at them as separate or real, like watching a magician's creations or a dream, yet realizing that these appearing phenomena nonetheless function in accord with the laws of cause and effect."

105

W̄hat is the excellent action
that embraces every goodness?
Rejoicing from the depths of one's heart
in the goodness of self and others.

The Seventh Dalai Lama concludes his series of verses on the
six perfections with this reference to the practice of always rejoicing in the goodness of self and others. He does this for a
number of reasons.

Firstly, rejoicing in the goodness, glory and successes of others is a force that prevents the arisal of jealousy. Jealousy easily
gives rise to anger and hatred, a main impediment to the
bodhisattva path. By always keeping the mind in the sphere of
rejoicing about others, this poison is eliminated.

Secondly, a great deal of strength and courage is required to
maintain the consistently positive application that is concomitant
with the bodhisattva practice of the six perfections. Rejoicing in
the goodness and merits of self and others reinforces the positive
within oneself and helps sustain this strength and courage.

Lama Tsongkhapa said, "Rejoicing is the singularly most
powerful practice, for it brings added power to every other application, eliminates many hindrances and increases our inner
joy. By means of it we are able to draw all the past, present and
future goodness of self and others directly into our lives."

106

What is the way to transcend
the indulgences of samsara and nirvana?
Turning one's back on self-centered thoughts
and arousing the bodhimind, the altruistic
wish for enlightenment.

Those who pursue the path to liberation and enlightenment must
avoid two main pitfalls: the attraction to indulgence in samsara,
or worldly glory; and the path to indulgence in nirvana, or transcendental joy. The bodhisattva aspiration, which is the basis of
the practice of the six perfections, helps one to avoid both of
these obstacles.

Maitreya Buddha said of the bodhisattva attitude, "Due to
the power of its wisdom it bestows protection from indulgence
in samsara, and due to the power of its compassion it bestows
protection from indulgence in solitary nirvana." The bodhisattva
wisdom realizes the void nature of the three circles: the one
practicing the path, the path being practiced, and the act of practice. Because of this, all the blissful experiences, extraordinary
powers and so forth that arise in meditation are seen as dreams,
illusions and magician's creations. This protects from indulgence
in samsara. Moreover, the great compassion that flows naturally for the illusory sentient beings cuts off the instinct of apathy and complacence and protects against mere nirvana. The
aspiration to highest enlightenment as a means of being of greatest benefit to living beings propels the practitioner past the abyss
of solitary nirvana to the very shores of full buddhahood itself.

The great Indian master Shantideva said, "When one relies
on a powerful protector, even one's greatest failings are par-
doned. Why then would an intelligent person not rely on the

bodhimind, for it brings swift release from all failings. Just like the fire at the end of the eon consumes the world, the bodhimind instantly and utterly burns all powerful negativities."

107

What are the legs and what the eyes
of those who travel to omniscience?
The varieties of spiritual methods are the legs;
and the eyes are the wisdom seeing the
ultimate mode of things.

With this verse the Seventh Dalai Lama pays homage to another of his Indian heroes, the master Acharya Chandrakirti,
clarifier of the emptiness doctrines of Nagarjuna. Chandrakirti
in his *magnum opus* entitled *A Guide to the Middle View*, or
Madhyamaka-avatara, a work the Seventh had studied in his youth
for three years, uses this metaphor to describe the manner in
which the six perfections carry a practitioner to enlightenment.
He likens the first five perfections—those of generosity, self-
discipline, patience, joyous effort and meditative absorption—to
the legs of the traveller, and likens the sixth perfection—that
of wisdom—to the eyes. He presents only a thumbnail sketch
of the first five perfections, and dedicates the main part of his
text to the perfection of wisdom, or the opening of the eyes
required for that journey. Nonetheless he stresses the importance of holding the two—method and wisdom—in balance in
one's own practice. To travel the long journey to the city of
enlightenment we need both strong legs and clear eyes.

Also in the same work Chandrakirti states, "The swan king
flies in front of the flock. His two broad white wings of conven-
tion (i.e., method) and thatness (i.e., wisdom) are spread wide.
Riding the powerful winds of great merit, he easily crosses the
ocean to enlightenment's excellence."

The Second Dalai Lama, who was wont to break out in mystical song, once intoned the following words in melody:

Ah oh la, the wise they sing, ya yi ya yi.

The wisdom of emptiness grasped by great compassion is the very essence of the Great Way.

Ah oh la, the wise they sing, ya yi ya yi.

This, practiced on the basis of the six perfections, is the mighty bodhisattva path itself.

Ah oh la, the wise they sing, ya yi ya yi.

It is method and wisdom combined; and through it the dance of great bliss and void comes to pervade one's every experience.

108

What is the one root of all
goodness in samsara and nirvana?
The clear light of one's own mind,
which by nature is free from every stain.

The basis of all conscious life is the mind, with its twofold quality of radiance and knowing. On its most subtle level, the mind
is pure luminosity, or primordial clear light. Maitreya likened
this aspect of the mind to the sky; the clouds of distortion and
the delusions move through the sky and sometimes even obstruct the light of the sun, but they cannot actually harm or
stain the sky. When conditions change, the clouds disappear and
the pure sky shines through in all its glory.

The essential nature of mind is equally pristine in all living
beings, from earthworms to buddhas. However, those on basic
levels of consciousness fall prey to the distortions and delusions because of misapprehending the nature of the self. Moved
by these factors they engage in negative behavior and bring suffering to self and others. Even the most seemingly evil person
has the primordial clear light mind at the heart of his or her
existence. Eventually the clouds of distortion and delusion will
be cleared away as the being grows in wisdom, and the evil behavior that emanates from these negative mind-sets will naturally evaporate. That being will realize the essential nature of
his or her own mind, and achieve spiritual liberation and enlightenment.

The Buddha said, "The world is led by the mind. All good
and evil deeds are created by it. It revolves like a fire wheel,
moves like waves, burns like a forest fire, and widens like a great
river."

As His Holiness the present Dalai Lama once put it, "The clear light mind, which lies dormant in living beings, is the great hope of mankind."

The Seventh Dalai Lama concludes his treatment of the path to enlightenment on this positive note. This is the final gem of wisdom that he offers us.

Dedication

What is delusional and what is not?
To show the difference I wrote this song
of useful hints from the tongues of sages,
arranged as a precious string of jewels.

By any merits it may have, may all beings
quickly attain to the state of Manjushri,
Bodhisattva of Wisdom. May they open the
eye of realization that sees what to transcend and what to cultivate; and may they
attain to the sublime state of inner knowledge and joy without end.

All Tibetan texts close with a verse (or several verses) of dedication. This was a literary tradition adopted from Buddhist India and continued over the centuries until the present day. The
Seventh Dalai Lama opened *Gems of Wisdom* with a verse of
homage to Manjushri, the bodhisattva symbolizing the wisdom
of the void; here he closes it with a verse of dedication to the
ideal that all living beings may attain to that same sublime state.

His statement, "I wrote this song of useful hints from the
tongues of sages," is his way of paying respect to all the great
Buddhist masters of the past whose lineages he received. He is
saying that his work is a re-phrasing of the instructions of these
great beings, and is not a mere invention or musing of his own
making. As the author, he is the artist who devised the form in
which his text is executed, but the basic paint with which he is
working is the timeless and perennial wisdom of the ages.

His aspiration is that all who read his composition may open
the eye of wisdom that sees what to transcend and what to cultivate, and thus attain to the sublime state of inner knowledge
and joy without end.

Printed in the United States
by Baker & Taylor Publisher Services